Design Techniques for
Modern Lace

Design Techniques for Modern Lace

Veronica D. Sorenson

B. T. Batsford Limited · London

This book is dedicated to Lynsey and Keri Neun. In Loving memory of two young lacemakers.

By the same author
Modern Lace Designs

ISBN 0 7134 6021 0

Filmset by Tradespools Ltd, Frome, Somerset
and printed in Britain by Butler and Tanner Ltd,
Frome, Somerset

for the publishers
B. T. Batsford Limited
4 Fitzhardinge Street
London W1H 0AH

Contents

1 · Introduction

This is primarily a book to assist any would-be designers of lace and to encourage them to take that first step. Once on their way, they will find ideas flowing more freely and the actual mechanics of producing a finished piece of lace from the original concept should become easier.

A number of prickings ready to be worked are included here, but many are incomplete and there are no very detailed working instructions as such, as a certain basic technical knowledge is assumed. This is partly to obtain the maximum use of available space but predominantly to encourage the lacemaker to study the design itself and to understand the methods and techniques used to attain it.

There are many sources of learning about the basic elements of design. Public libraries stock numerous books which can be borrowed, and classes are held in Design and Art at many Local Authority Adult Education Colleges, whilst weekend workshops are available at residental colleges. An awareness of good and bad design can be gained by taking note of our everyday surroundings and looking at the district in which we live when out shopping or walking the dog. Television, for example series on various textiles, can also stimulate this awareness. Even reading the back of cereal packets at the breakfast table and dissecting the advertising and artwork found on them can increase our comprehension of, and insight into, colour, shape and the composition of a design.

It is also possible to purchase books which contain sketches and many ideas for designs. These are specially published with the intention of being used by artists and designers of all crafts. By using such books and, perhaps taking a bit from one and a bit from another, a first design can be produced. After this, more original ideas will gradually emerge and you can become far more adventurous in your work.

When using and adapting designs and shapes originating in past centuries, the question of copyright does not usually occur, but, frequently, unknown to one another and working independently, designers concurrently have similar ideas and their finished patterns are very alike. This perhaps suggests the possibility of plagiarism, but this is seldom (if ever) an intentional act, and rather the parallel workings of like minds. If a designer is unsure, it is far better to abandon the development of any pattern if the intention is to sell the finished pricking. Remember that it is allowable to make one copy of any pattern for one's own personal use, but as soon as further copies are made and these are passed around or sold, the probability of being in breach of copyright law is very real. Once the copyright has lapsed, however, it is reasonably safe to do this. Indeed, in this way, a design can sometimes be kept alive to become a traditional one which does not fade into obscurity.

Every designer develops his or her own particular style with its own trade mark and it is usually possible instantly to recognise their work. This book reflects strongly my own style but anyone using these ideas will naturally put into their own work an extra *je ne sais quoi* which will give it its individuality. The basic rules of design must always be obeyed. It is the treatment and development of any first thoughts within this necessary framework which reflect the personality of the designer and produce the unique features of each new design.

Above all, do not be afraid to have a go. If (or rather when) you produce a failure, it is not the end of the world, and you have gained knowledge in the realization of this failure. It is not normal for any of us to produce a piece of pure genius at the first attempt. Most good designers have files full of the failures which preceded just one excellent piece of work. You can only develop your own ability through investigation, experimentation and involvement with the subject. So what, if you cannot draw and were thrown out of the Art class at school? There are very few of us who are ignorant of the techniques of using tracing paper, and modern photostat machines are more than able to cope with demands for reducing shapes or enlarging them to any required dimensions.

Although this book is divided into chapters, it is impossible to separate the elements of design into rigid compartments. Therefore, the reader will probably need to refer to several sections in the book when producing a new design or pattern.

I would like to apologise to any person of the male gender who reads and uses this book. The use of 'she' and 'her' when making reference to the lacemaker/designer is purely a convenience as the majority of them are indeed female. I am no feminist and no offence is intended towards the gentlemen laceworkers amongst us.

May I wish you all well in your endeavours, and hope that this volume will give you hours of pleasure and may assist you in your search for fulfilment in the development of your designing skills.

I would like to thank Norma Hanstead for her patience in ploughing through the manuscript and Dick Chenery for his hours of dedicated work in producing the photographs in this book. Also, I must express my gratitude to my family, friends and students who must, by now, be heartily sick and tired of the word 'lace', and yet still come up with more outrageous designs for me to attempt!

2 · What is design?

In the *Concise Oxford English Dictionary*, the definition of 'design' contains a variety of phrases to explain what seems, on the surface, a very simple word. Some of these are: mental plan; delineation; pattern; artistic or literary groundwork; general idea; construction; plot; invention; and, as a verb, contrive; plan, and purpose. It can be seen from this list that design can be explained in a variety of ways, but essentially a design is a preliminary outline, to be constructed, developed and worked at a later date by the designer or by another person. It is, then, an amalgamation of all these definitions. No one thing produces a design. It is a combination of different factors which are united to present an overall picture.

It is much easier to produce a bad design than a good one. A sketch of any outline of an idea can be prepared at very short notice and with the minimum of time and effort, but this does not necessarily make it a good design or even one that is workable in the medium for which it is intended. Very occasionally, an excellent pattern can be thus produced, but normally the original idea must be worked upon, left for a while, developed and improved again and again, before a final workable pattern emerges.

There are many designs which can be worked in a number of different mediums with very satisfactory results. A pattern can be intended to be worked in embroidery, for instance, while the basic shape is also capable of being crocheted, or made in tapestry or in bobbin lace; but the medium for which it was originally intended usually produces the best results. However, it is frequently possible, with a little adaptation and some forethought, to produce a very good design for another technique based on the original shape. This possibility will be discussed later, always bearing in mind any copyright that may be in existence on the original pattern.

Throughout the ages, designs have always reflected the era during which the originator has lived. Thus, for example, the shapes within the patterns originating in Tudor times are distinctive and completely different from those produced in the Regency period. Likewise, the patterns being made today inevitably reflect the way in which we live and the materials available to us. So it is that we should be able to leave our mark on the history of design, so that in one or two hundred years' time people will be able to associate and identify the designs being produced in the late 1900s as typical of our age.

A good design is visually pleasing to the eye in a number of ways. These must all blend together harmoniously to give an overall feeling of pleasure and of a unified entity. The elements which combine together in order to achieve this effect can be listed as follows:

1 Texture
2 Form or shape
3 Colour
4 Proportion
5 Space

Bad designs are ugly and it is usually very difficult to recognise the various elements within them. Instead they tend to conflict with and counteract one another. Bad designs are nearly always the product of lack of training, carelessness and slipshod work which has been produced in a great hurry, with very little forethought given to the finished product and effect. Most designers can improve the quality of their work with a little more study of the basic and important factors involved in producing a

Fig. 1. *A design in the making: some of the drawing instruments and materials required*

design. These few guidelines may be helpful for a would-be designer before she makes a start.

1 Every element listed above should be taken into consideration before attempting to put pen to paper – or thread to bobbin. It is not sufficient to make a decision on the overall shape, without considering where and how the finished product is to be used, what colour or colours (if any) are needed to enhance it, and which threads will be the best to use.

2 A design must fulfil the purpose for which it is intended. It is not desirable to produce a

beautiful, very intricate and minute pattern for a wall-hanging that is meant to be viewed from a distance, because, if this is done, a pair of binoculars will probably be required to see the finished lace. Conversely, a large shape worked in very thick thread would prove disastrous for a paperweight design or a handkerchief edge. These are, of course, very extreme instances, but they demonstrate the point that a little thought at this stage of a design will soon prove to be beneficial and time-saving.

3 The materials that make up any piece of work must be suited to its purpose. It is not advisable to use a very fine silken thread when making a tablecloth that needs frequent laundering, for example. A thicker linen thread would be far more practical, while the fine silk would be most desirable for a delicate lace edging intended for use on underwear, or for a Christening gown.

4 A good design will always merge into its surroundings to give an overall pleasing effect, rather than sticking out like a sore thumb. In a room already decorated in a contemporary style with simple lines and a muted colour scheme, a picture in the Victorian idiom would certainly not be displayed to its maximum advantage. It would be far better to produce a design with a very simple shape using exquisite stitchery and suitable colour tones to obtain the desired effect.

5 The basic outline and inside shapes must be instantly discernible. Whether it is a conventional, photographic type representation, or an abstract, symbolic motif, a good design is uncluttered. The outline of a painted or embroidered shape can be made far more detailed by using fine brush strokes or stitches to produce an irregular impression, but this is not advisable in bobbin lace due to the stringencies of the medium. An attempt at this sort of outline would end in abysmal failure. It is far better to iron out any bumps and to produce a smooth, even effect. Any intentional irregularities can be indicated by the use of suitable stitches or changes of colour.

6 There must be 'movement' in any design. This is the ability to draw an onlooker's eye smoothly over the completed piece of work. Each element should flow gradually from one to the other. As a Hogarth curve is used by Floral Art devotees to bring movement to an arrangement, so lace designers can use similar techniques in their work. A piece of lace should

give the impression of fluidity and lightness even if it is in reality fixed to a solid and immoveable object.

7 All the various elements must be linked by a common theme. It is not advisable to put a triangular shape in one corner and round lines throughout the rest of the pattern. This would separate the one corner and prevent it from becoming an integral part of the design. By using either all angular or all curved lines, a more integrated and pleasing overall effect would be achieved. The same type of shape should be incorporated into the design throughout, in order to link the various elements into an entity.

8 Colour is frequently necessary to give a piece of work vitality and life, but do not fall into the trap of believing that a piece of work must have colour simply because it is fashionable! If any colours are used, they must blend harmoniously, not only with one another, but with any area that surrounds the finished piece of work. It is not essential to use a large number of different colours within a particular pattern. Frequently, a blend of tones of one colour is sufficient, and even preferable, in order to achieve the effect of depth and texture within the work. If one colour only is used, the stitches themselves and their arrangement must give the desired effect. It is occasionally possible to use discordant colours to great effect, but this should preferably be attempted only by a person trained and skilled in the use of colour. A thorough knowledge of the colour wheel and primary and secondary colours, and of all the subtle blending that can be achieved, is essential.

9 A good design allows for plenty of space within the outline as well as outside it. Where there is any solid area of work, make it stand out by putting 'air' around it or give the stitches around it a very open texture. Many excellent designs have been spoiled by the haphazard and indiscriminate use of filling stitches which clutter up the pattern. It is not necessary to 'show off' a number of complicated manoeuvres with the threads. A really first-rate pattern will make use of these stitches only if they enhance the work and there is enough room to display them to advantage. If there is only a small area of work within a solid section of the design, it is far better to use a simple open-work stitch or even to leave it blank, so that the important basic shape itself is clearly visible.

10 It is vitally important that the proportions of any design are correct. Proportion is the ratio of one object to another. If a design is badly proportioned, the overall effect is distorted, but good proportions enhance a design. This balance must be struck so that the finished piece of work is not top heavy, nor is one particular area too empty or too overcrowded. In the same way, the proportions of a framed piece of work should be attractive. The motif must fill a sufficient area of the backing so that

the space around it is not too large, making the motif itself appear as a dot on the horizon!

Similarly, when designing an edging for a garment, one that is too wide or too narrow can detract from the original intention of attractive decoration: it will either take over or be lost. This also applies to the design within the actual lace edging. A tiny section of whole stitch with a large amount of ground is insubstantial, in the same way that a solid design with very few ground stitches becomes clumsy and heavy.

Having discussed the basic elements of design, now is the time to work some exercises in order to assimilate and bring together these ideas. Each of the following sections deals with a particular type of finished lace and the various textures and coloured threads available to the modern lacemaker. It is to be hoped that some of the patterns produced by a designer adopting these ideas will be recognised as typical designs of the latter part of the twentieth century, in the same way as the traditional patterns being made today reflect the age in which they were first designed.

3 · Braid lace design

This type of lace is frequently called 'tape lace' but I consider this to be something of a misnomer, since this description really belongs to those laces made with a needle, thread and lengths of ready-made machine tape. In the late 1800s, tape lace was often known as 'modern', and much was produced in order to try to combat the encroachment of the machine-made varieties and to attempt to keep the hand-made lace industry alive. Needless to say, history proved this impossible, although nowadays many shops in Europe do sell work of this type which is currently being produced. Therefore, I consider it preferable to separate the two principal ways of producing bobbin laces into continuous and sectional, thus eliminating this problem, and to call the bobbin-made variety 'braid lace'.

Braid, or sectional, lace is frequently regarded as the poor relation of the continuous lace which needs many pairs of bobbins to complete it. This is rather unfortunate as attractive shapes of sheer simplicity can be worked using either colour or a variety of stitches, and this can produce very practical yet beautiful laces if the designer puts a little thought into them.

The foremost continuous laces being made today in the traditional manner are of the Torchon, Bucks Point, Beds/Maltese and Flanders types. Many modern designs originating in Europe are also continuous but they adapt and combine the traditional techniques with modern threads and shapes and cannot come under these established headings.

The sectional laces are predominantly Honiton, Bruges Flower Work, Russian Tape Lace and Schneeberg Lace. These are formed by working the basic design with a bobbin braid and then using bobbins to make fillings with a variety of stitches, thus uniting the various elements. Many lacemakers who decry 'tape' lace, but specialize in Honiton lace techniques, are horrified to be told that they are, in fact, producing tape lace - another reason for my preference of the word 'sectional' or 'braid'. The majority of Italian and East European laces have also traditionally been produced in this manner, as well as the Brussels and Duchesse laces – two of the most beautiful.

I am often asked to put my designs into categories, but many of them defy such classification as they are a mixture of a number of different techniques. I have heard this sort of work called 'bastard', 'mixed' or 'combination' lace, but none of these terms really do justice to this type of lace, which can be really beautiful.

There are any number of modern braid lace designs available for purchase which are really excellent; 'modern' should not mean 'shoddy' or 'slapdash' – unfortunately one sometimes sees some rather carelessly produced prickings. They do not always reflect that the originator has in fact put much effort into the pattern and make it appear to be nothing but scribbled doodles. It can be very confusing to attempt to work a pricking where the pin-holes are not marked with precision and the working lines are carelessly drawn. As much care must be taken to produce a good sectional lace pricking as one that is based on graph paper with rigidly set rules and ready-made hole positions.

It is not as easy as it may appear to produce a good simple lace pricking. Often more thought than is generally presumed is needed as regards the relationship between the thickness of thread used and the distance between the pin-holes, in order to produce a substantial piece of work which has qualities of beauty and endurance. Thus, many lacemakers are discouraged from learning to design, and even work, simple sectional laces, merely because the effect of the finished work has been poor and unattractive in the past.

Although many doodles can be transcribed into workable pieces of lace, frequently just one of these could be isolated and used as a repetitive design or even as a single motif to better effect. A simple shape may appear easy to draw but it is very necessary to put great care into curved lines to ensure that the curves are not bumpy and have a very clean, smooth finish. This can be readily achieved with the use of simple drawing instruments and not by relying entirely on the eye and free-hand sketching. It must be remembered that practically all bobbin lace originates on a piece of graph paper. Do not worry that Drawing and Geometry were not your favourite subjects at school. There are a few simple rules that can be understood and easily learned by the worst mathematician or Art student, and once followed, they will help to provide a basis for good braid lace design.

These rules have been applied to the designs in this section and will be explained as appropriate. Firstly, it would be of advantage if the following exercise is worked through, so that an appreciation of the techniques of simple braid lace design can be formed, and the required tools can be handled correctly. For this exercise, a piece of graph paper, a pair of compasses or a radius curve, an eraser and a ruler are all the tools that are required.

Exercise in drawing connecting circles

1 Draw two rows of circles, each having the same radius, making sure that the centres of the circles in each row lie in a straight line on the graph paper and are the same distance apart (*see* diagram 1*a*).

Diag. 1. *Drawing connecting circles*

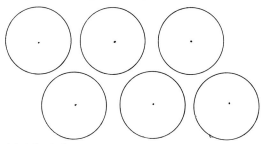

(*a*) *The circles*

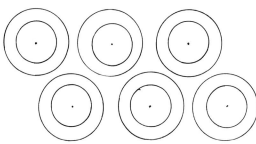

(*b*) *Double circles*

(*c*) *Marking the tangents*

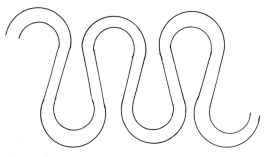

(*d*) *The finished shape*

2 Using the same centre holes, draw a smaller circle inside each of the ones already drawn, ensuring that the distance between the inner and outer circles is the required width of the finished braid (*see* diagram 1*b*).

3 Now draw tangents from the top row of circles to the bottom row, joining the outside top circles to the inside bottom circles and vice versa (*see* diagram 1*c*).

4 The superfluous parts of the circles and tangents can now be erased. A regular wavy shape is left with a constant distance between the lines (*see* diagram 1*d*).

Pin-hole positions

The next stage is to mark the pin-hole positions. They are determined by the thickness of thread to be used. The exact distance is best calculated by working a small tension sample, but an approximation which can be used as a starting point is as follows:

> Bockens/BOUC 50 linen threads need a distance between the pin-holes of 5mm; DMC Fil à Dentelle 70 or 80 needs 3mm; DMC Brillante d'Alsace 30 needs 2mm.

The most important thing to remember is that the pin-hole distances are measured on the *outside* line round the curves and that this

Diag. 2. *Positioning pin-holes*

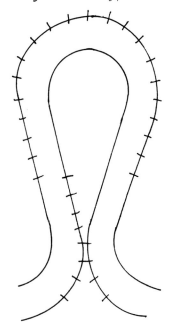

(a) *Marking the outer line of the braid*

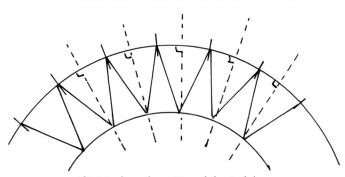

(b) *Marking the position of the pin holes*

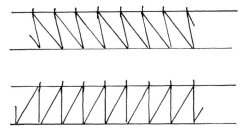

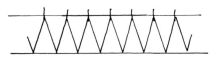

(c) *Drawing the lines for worker threads: left, incorrect; right, correct*

distance remains constant throughout the piece of lace. The inside pin-holes will take care of themselves. Make a small dash across the outline in preference to marking a dot (*see* diagram 2*a*). This gives a clearer indication of position and the pin-hole will be placed where this dash crosses the outline. If these marks are not equidistant, the finished lace will have an uneven and untidy edge. It is vital to have sufficient pin-holes round the outside of any curve for several reasons, amongst which are to prevent the passives from creeping into the inner edge, and to give a firm, tidy edge to the work.

Marking the pin-holes on the inner line is quite simple once the basic principle of braid lace is understood. It is very important that the lines for the worker threads travel forwards all the time and do not slope backwards (*see* diagram 2*c*). To ensure this, imagine a right-angle dropped from half-way between the marks on the outside curved line to the inner line. The place where these cross will be the point where the inner pin-hole will be marked (*see* diagram 2*b*). The working lines can now be drawn on the pattern. These will make small V shapes from the outer line to the inner one. Do not worry that the inner pin-holes are closer together than the outer ones. There are a number of ways of dealing with this problem in order to prevent the lace from buckling and to keep it neat and smooth.

Cuff design

The simple cuff pattern (pricking 1) is designed on the above principle. The pattern as it stands fits an adult wrist comfortably and looks most effective as a decoration on a blouse or dress with a wide cuff. If it is necessary to make it larger, the pattern repeat can be worked as many times as necessary.

For this pattern, BOUC 50 Fil de Lin thread

Pricking 1. *Simple Braid Lace Cuff*

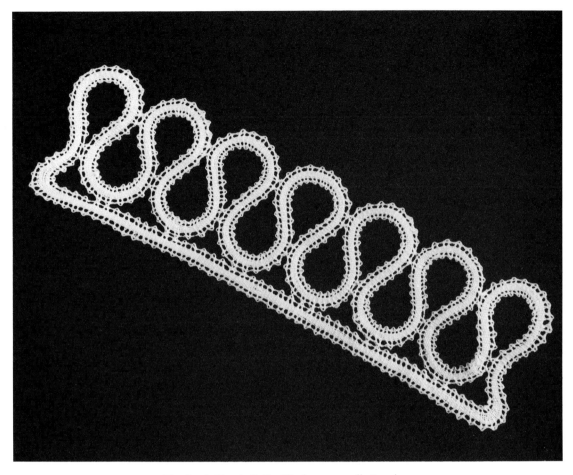

Fig. 2. A *Simple Cuff – this has a very effective shape*

was used and seven pairs of bobbins were needed. The braid is worked in whole stitch with the outside passive pairs worked in whole stitch and twist. Twist the worker pair once before working the outside passive pairs and twice round the pin.

Collar pattern

This simple design can be extended if polar graph paper is used instead of ordinary graph paper. By studying the second pattern which is worked using the same thread as the first, it can be seen that the circles are formed into a ring instead of a straight line. It is necessary to give the outer circles a larger radius than the inner ones because the radiating lines of the graph paper become wider further away from the centre point. This means, of course, that there is a much larger empty space within the outer circles. This can partly be filled by moving the centre of the inside circle towards the centre spot, thus widening the braid at this place. By changing the stitches to whole stitch and twist from whole stitch only, it is not necessary to add more passives to the work and the finished lace is still firm.

Once the basic shape has been drawn, it can be seen that the area within the circles is too great to leave completely blank. If a fancy filling were to be used, this would detract from the beauty

Pricking 2. *Collar to complement the Cuff*

of the curved shapes, so a simple, yet fairly rigid, filling is required, It is not always a good idea to work a traditional plait and picot filling in a piece of lace that might need frequent laundering because this could become ragged and tatty quite easily. Therefore, a filling of tallies can be very useful. These respond to laundering quite well providing they are executed with care and they also give an impression of solidity in the space without needing too many extra pairs of bobbins. In this particular case, it would be a weakening feature if there were too many starts and finishes with a number of knotted endings, so the filling can be

worked either while the basic braid is being constructed, or afterwards. Only four extra pairs of bobbins are required and the threads can be carried across the back of the work invisibly at the majority of the joining places, this reducing the number of endings required.

The particular design which illustrates this point was used as a collar on a dress but it can also be worked as a round mat edging by working 18 complete repeats of pattern. It will be noticed that this 'collar' does not reach round the entire neck edge of the garment. This is because the back of this dress was an odd shape and it was more convenient to end the

Fig. 3. A Collar Design – *this complements the cuff. Note how the outline of the lace follows the line of the dress yoke and the shapes on the material are echoed in the tallies*

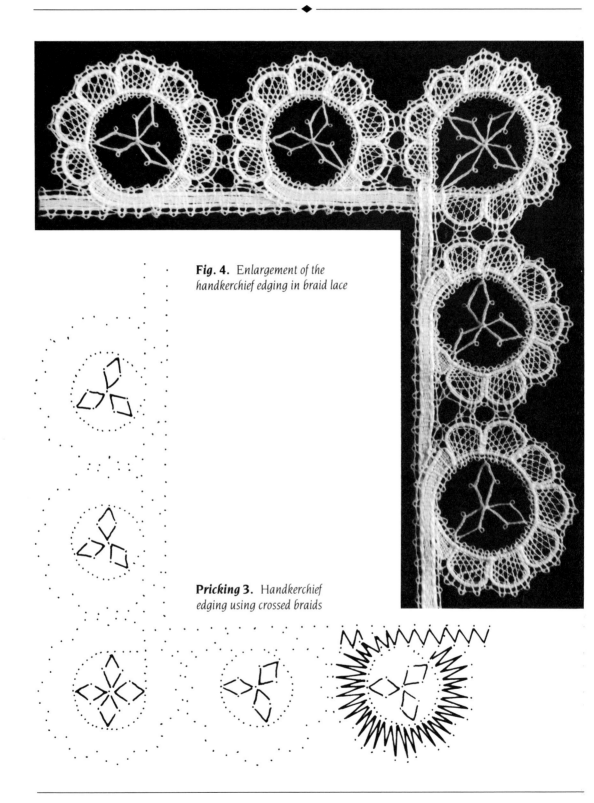

Fig. 4. *Enlargement of the handkerchief edging in braid lace*

Pricking 3. *Handkerchief edging using crossed braids*

lace at the shoulder seam. This is a good idea for other neck edges because designing collars can be a very tricky business. So often, a garment has a neck edge which is so shaped that the proposed lace collar design will not lie flat across the back of the nape of the neck. The dress or blouse should always be prepared first, before any lace collar is made, so that a design template can be prepared and adjusted before many hours of work are wasted. When comparing collar patterns, it can be readily seen that there is a large variety of neck shapings. A very slight variation in shape can be the difference between disaster and a beautiful piece of work which enhances the garment for which it was intended.

Crossing braids

Now is the time to experiment with braid shapes that cross one another. Once again, draw a simple row of circles first, but this time ensure that they touch one another. They can now be turned into a continuous looped shape (see pricking 3). This is worked using seven pairs of bobbins wound with BOUC 120 Fil de Lin, and two single bobbins using DMC Coton Perlé 5. To make the design more interesting, each loop has been extended to form a simple flower shape based on Bruges flowers. The two gimp threads have been introduced in the same way as for Honiton lace, and the centre section of the braid is worked in whole stitch but changed to half stitch for the petals.

Designing corners

Corners can be a little problematic when designing braid laces as there is a square of space to be filled which normally will not accommodate a design which has travelled quite happily along a straight edge. Frequently, loops have to be stretched into oblong shapes or extra small loops must be inserted to fit the

shape. It is worthwhile practising the design of corners on graph paper to discover the different effects that can be obtained.

Intertwined braid shapes

The inspiration for braid lace designs can originate from a number of sources. Many patterns intended to be worked in another medium have small sections which can be adapted. Amongst the Celtic archives can be found a wealth of interesting intertwined and sophisticated shapes. The *Book of Kells*, which is to be found in the Trinity College in Dublin, was written over 1000 years ago and is beautifully illustrated by the monks of the time. There is a multitude of intricate shapes contained within it which can be translated into exquisite laces. The 'Ring of Eternity' (pricking 4) is one such pattern and it has a fascinating structure to work upon. This pattern can be made using DMC Fil à Dentelle thread colour 954 and seven pairs of bobbins for each braid. Each ring is fully intertwined with the others, with no ends or beginnings. It looks very simple at first glance, but the working of it becomes quite complex. It is impossible to work a complete section of braid without a break. The numerous other

Diag. 3. *Braid weaving for the twelfth century motif*

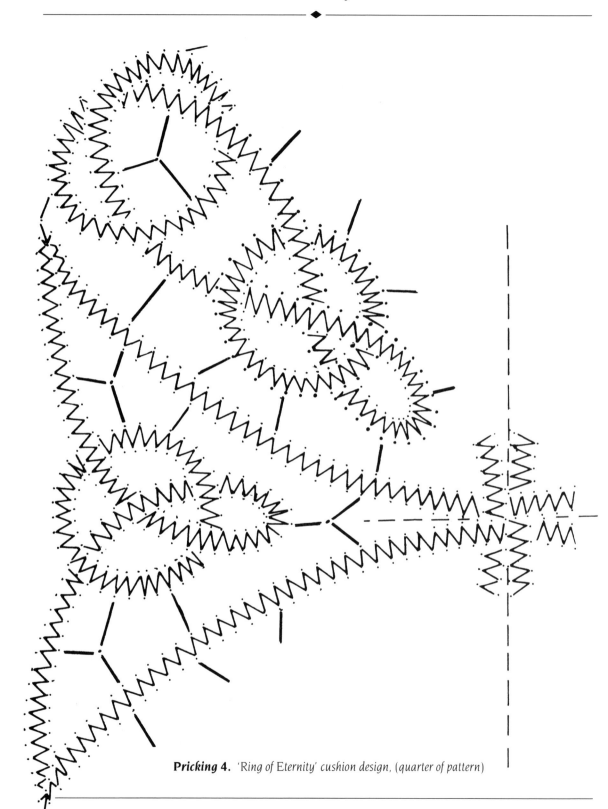

Pricking 4. 'Ring of Eternity' cushion design, (quarter of pattern)

◆

shapes found within each illuminated page in this book make a very interesting study, especially when you recall its antiquity and the lack of modern sophisticated drawing instruments available for use by the artists.

The second pricking, illustrating an intertwined motif (pricking 5), appears simple at first glance. But here we find straight line shapes combining with circles and loops. The pattern originated on the Counterseal of Roger de Lasci, who was the Constable of Chester between 1179 and 1211, thus making it a little

more recent than the shapes from the *Book of Kells*. When working the lace, each braid needs eight pairs of bobbins wound with BOUC 50 Fil de Lin. To make the sections distinctive from one another, try using different tones of thread for each. For example, the inner ring can be wound in unbleached linen thread, the next looped shape in half-bleach and the outer square in white. This has the effect of darkening the centre and gradually lightening the work to the outside.

Fig. 5. *Twelfth-century motif, with intertwined braids of different shapes and tones of one colour*

Pricking 5. *Twelfth-century motif (half of design)*

Fig. 6. *Mat consisting of various different-textured braids*

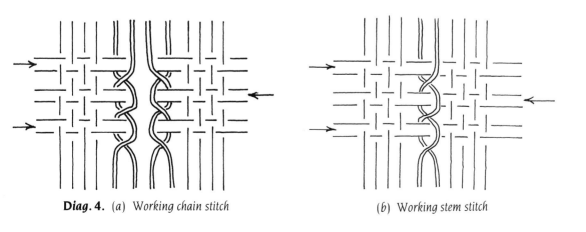

Diag. 4. (*a*) *Working chain stitch*   (*b*) *Working stem stitch*

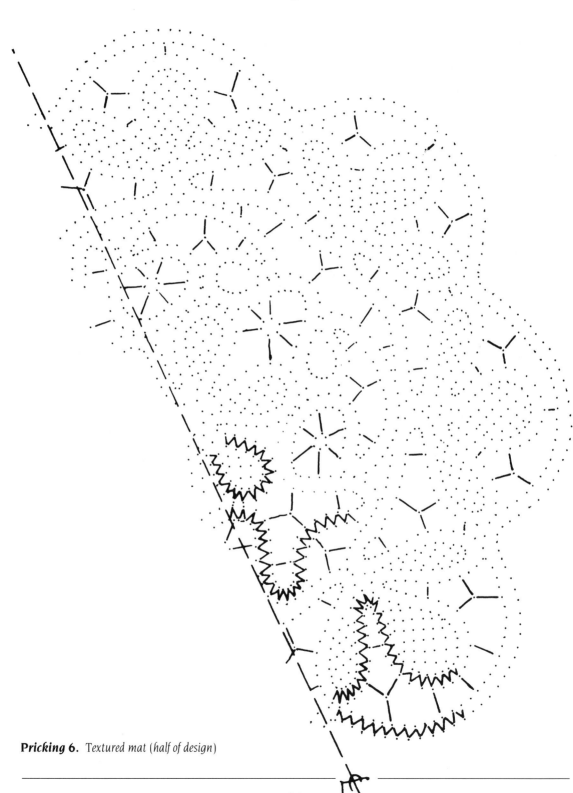

Pricking 6. Textured mat (half of design)

Textured braids

Pricking 6 is included to encourage experiment with textured braids. Chain stitch and stem stitch produce a raised effect which is assisted by the fact that the thread used for these is a lighter colour than that used for the main thread (see diagram 4). Those used here are BOUC 90 Fil de Lin unbleached and DMC Coton Perlé in ecru. The separate braids only touch one another: they do not cross and each is worked slightly differently to the others. In addition, the actual shape of each and the number of repeats are not constant. It is very interesting to experiment with changing shapes in this way.

The seemingly haphazard doodle of the central braid has assisted in producing an attractive mat. The curves of this were adjusted to complement the regular sections. Great care must be taken to avoid any sharp corners or awkwardly shaped curves. Notice, too, that only some of the more definite shapes have fillings. This makes them more prominent within the design, while the rest of the braids are merely joined with false plaits, to prevent the whole structure from falling apart when removed from the pillow.

4 · Schneeberg lace

Schneeberg lace can truly be called 'modern'. It was developed at the beginning of the twentieth century by a small group of designers and teachers at the lace school in Schneeberg, a town in the southern part of Germany. This school was originally called the Royal Bobbin Lace Design School; then its name was changed to the Barbara Uttmann School, and nowadays it is known as the Technical School of Applied Art. The necessity for a simplified form of lacemaking came about because of the rise of the machine lace industry and the desire to keep the hand-made lace industry alive. Unfortunately, we cannot obtain any of the original designs but the techniques have been passed down via ex-students and teachers at this school.

As this type of lace will be relatively unfamiliar to some readers, some basic instruction as to the reading of the patterns is required. There are also a number of techniques in Schneeberg lace which may well be unfamiliar to lacemakers who are used to working solely traditional laces. Therefore, a short description of some of them is given in order that this type of lace is worked in the correct manner. Needless to say, these techniques are only basic and more advanced methods of working cannot be included here.

Reading the pattern

The basic braid of Schneeberg lace is normally worked using only four pairs of bobbins (three passive pairs and one worker pair). It is permissible to use one extra passive pair but there are never more than four passives. Half stitch is not usually found in the braid which is worked in either whole stitch or whole stitch

and twist. The area where the braid is worked in whole stitch and twist is indicated by a central line drawn on the pattern.

The work is commenced at a place where the shape becomes narrow. As the width increases, so the worker pair is twisted a greater number of times. The middle line on the pricking denotes the position of the central twisted passive pair on completion of the work. The other two passives are worked so that they lie at the edge of the braid just inside the pins. Where there is a second line at the outside of the pattern, a plait is worked using two extra pairs of bobbins. This plait joins and leaves the main braid so that it jumps across sections of the pattern like a bridge, but forms a continuous line round the edge of the lace with picots at intervals on the 'bridges' where they are long enough. This not only gives strength to the finished work, but also produces a firm, neat edge.

Commencing work

Work is always commenced at a point where a section of whole stitch braid is to be worked. This is necessary in order to make the finishing join invisible on the right side of the work. There are a number of different ways of effecting this in order to achieve the correct end product of a straight line. I find that the following method is the simplest to work (see diagram 5).

Hang the worker and passive pairs on a support pin which is placed a little above the start line. The worker pair must be at one end. Work a half stitch, pin, two over three with the worker pair and each of the other passives in turn, putting the pins in at regular intervals along the start line. Twist the worker pair twice and put in the last pin at the end of the row.

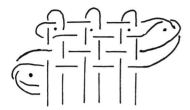

Diag. 5. *Commencing the braid in Schneeberg lace*

Take out the support pin and pull the threads down evenly to make a straight line.

The work can now be continued in whole stitch with the worker always twisting twice at each end of the row round the pin.

The edge plait

Where the edge plait joins the the braid, the worker pair from the braid makes a whole stitch through each of the two pairs of the plait in turn. A pin is placed inside all three pairs and the innermost pair is then used as the worker pair, across the main braid and back to the next outer pin position. When this point is reached, leave the worker pair and continue the plait which has been left at the previous outer pin, until it is long enough to reach the next pin-hole. Now the worker pair can make two whole stitches across the plait and the pin can be inserted as before (see diagram 6). There must be only one twist of the worker pair between the outside passive pair and the plait, however many twists have been worked between the

other two passives, in order to ensure that the outside passive pair lies directly on top of the inner of the two outside lines on the pattern.

Finishing the work

When the work has been completed and the braid rejoins its commencement, sewings are worked in the normal manner so that each pair of passives joins up with the place where it commences, but it is not always necessary to sew in the worker pair. Now split the pairs into two groups of two pairs each. For each of these groups, take one of the threads and make three or four buttonhole stitches round the other three threads (see diagram 7). Now make a sewing with this thread through the fabric of the braid, taking up only one thread, and then continue to make two or three more buttonhole stitches. This keeps the group of threads permanently under the braid and they will not be visible on the right side of the finished lace. Work the other set of threads in a similar fashion. The two bunches of anchored threads can now be cut short.

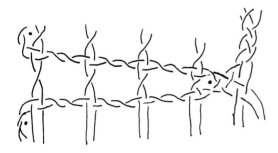

Diag. 6. *Working the edge plait in Schneeberg lace*

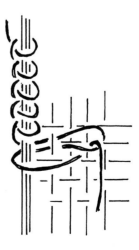

Diag. 7. *Finishing the threads in a bundle*

Working a centre filling

Two extra pairs of bobbins are needed for this particular filling. They are hung on at the place indicated on the pattern. This is point A on

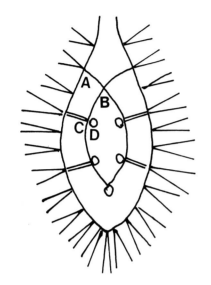

(a)

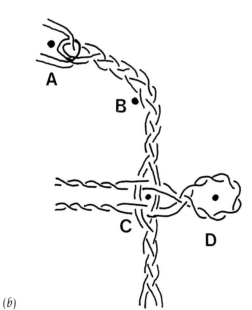

(b)

Diag. 8. (a) *Pricking for a plait and picot filling*
(b) *Working the filling*

diagram 8. Work a plait as far as C, putting in a support pin at B. Now continue the braid until the place for joining the plait and braid worker pair is reached. Twist the worker pair three times and make a three-pair crossing with this and the two pairs of the plait. Put in pin C between the two pairs of the plait and work a double picot with the worker pair only (pin D). When making this picot, use a pin that is slightly thicker than those used for the rest of the work. Another three-pair crossing is now worked with the worker pair and the plait pairs and the worker twisted three times. Before continuing the main braid, work the plait as far as the next pin-hole and leave it ready for use. This ensures that the worker pair will remain firmly in place and that the plait will be tight.

Continue in this way until the last pin-hole of the filling has been completed and work the plait as far as the support pin B. Make a sewing over the original plait at this place and then continue the plait to its finishing position. When the braid reaches this point, the plait will be joined in as per the instructions for crossing plaits and braids. If it is not to be carried across the work, it will be finished as per the instructions for finishing braids by working buttonhole stitches.

Crossing plaits and braids

There are two main methods of working these, depending upon the position of the crossing places on the pricking. The lacemaker must determine for herself which of these methods will be necessary for the pattern in question. It is far better to carry the threads across the back of the work than to finish off and restart, as the latter method makes for a weaker piece of lace and more ends to conceal.

For the first method of crossing, the workers leave the braid at the pin-hole before the one where the plait joins the work (see diagram 9a). A pin is then placed between the two pairs of the plait where they meet the braid, and the top pair is used as a worker pair across the braid to the pin-hole where the original worker has been left. The pin is placed between these two pairs and the plait leaving the braid is worked with them. The second pair of the plait entering the braid is now used as the new worker pair.

The second method is used when the plait entering the braid will leave it at a point further down, which has not yet been reached. The worker pair makes a three-pair crossing with the pairs from the plait (see diagram 9*b*) and the pin is positioned between the two pairs of the plait.

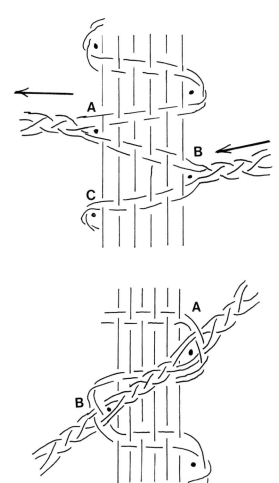

Diag. 9. *Two methods of crossing braids and plaits*

The plait is now continued to the place where it will leave the braid and is left for the time being. The braid is then worked keeping the original worker pair at the same place. Now the plait is brought into position; the pin put in between the two pairs of the plait, and a three-pair crossing made with the worker pair and the pairs of the plait. Both the plait and the braid can now be continued.

Turning corners

When a pattern indicates a sharp corner on the braid and there would not be sufficient space for all the pins at the inner edge of the curve, it is necessary to work a turning stitch. This type of stitch is found in all sectional laces, but each variety has its own particular movement which does not always work with other types of braid lace. For example, the back-stitching in Honiton lace and the method of working a pin twice in Bruges Flower Work are similar in effect but different in execution. For Schneeberg lace, the turning stitch is made as follows (see diagram 10).

Work to the place where the turning stitch is required. At this point the inside pair of passives will not be used. Make a movement of half-stitch, twist, two over three using the centre passive pair and the workers, and insert a pin to support both pairs of bobbins (*see* diagram 10*b*). The worker pair should now be in the position where it started. Continue the work as before but take out the support pin after a little more braid has been worked and gently ease the centre passive pair into the correct position. It should now lie in a smooth line and the pin position at the turning point should be invisible. When working a whole stitch and twist braid, though, obviously it will not be invisible. If the lacemaker working this movement has been used to the Continental method terminology, the turning stitch is worked by cross, twist, twist, cross.

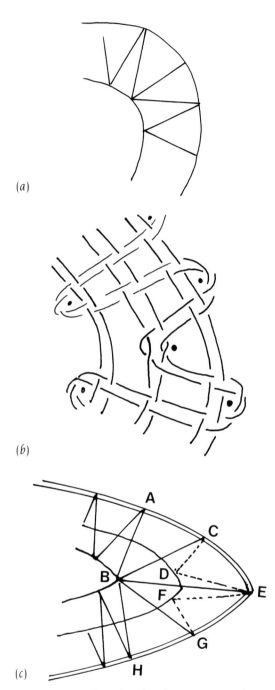

(a)

(b)

(c)

A

C

B   D

F   E

G

H

Diag. 10. *Working the Schneeberg turning stitch*
    (a) *Marking on the pattern*
    (b) *Position of the threads and pins*
    (c) *Working diagram for very sharp corners*

If the corner is so acute that several of these stitches must be worked (*see* diagram 10c), the turning stitch is worked at D and F. After working pin G, the worker pair goes back to B and a sewing is made into the loop formed when working it the first time, before continuing the braid.

Designing Schneeberg lace

Many shapes from the world of natural history, in the forms of animals, birds, butterflies and flowers, can be interpreted in a lace of this type. It gives rise to a wealth of ideas for creating beautiful shapes using curved lines. There are not usually many very angular shapes within Schneeberg patterns, although some geometrical patterns can be created, but fluid, curvaceous lines produce some exquisite laces.

Colour can be introduced with great ease to enhance the finished product, with very attractive results. By using three or four tones of one colour, some very interesting shading effects are produced. Each of the three passive pairs is wound in a different tone. They are hung on so that the lightest is positioned to the outside of the work and the darkest is at the inside. The three worker pairs are all wound in the middle tone only. It is better not to use multicoloured variegated threads as these detract from the overall shape and pattern. Another interesting devlopment is to use metallized threads either for all the passive pairs or for the centre passives only. If the metallized thread is the same colour as the other threads, the finished lace is given an attractive shine, but a gold or silver pair can be introduced when using all white main threads, which also gives the lace a 'lift'.

The patterns shown here are intended to give some insight into the basic working techniques in order that a future designer can then make patterns of her own. There are a number of refinements which cannot be included in the space available, as this is only meant as an introduction to this very lovely and adaptable lace form.

Tension plays a very important part in producing good lace and never more so than when working Schneeberg lace. If the plaits and picots are not worked tightly and evenly, a slovenly appearance is obtained, and if there are not enough twists of the workers in the wider sections of braid, they will become wobbly when the lace is removed from the pillow. Another unique feature is that, although the distance between the pin-holes must remain the same for the narrow sections of the braid, as it widens, this distance becomes greater to accommodate the twists and to allow for the curves which are an integral part of this type of lace. It is very useful to draw a sketch of an outline with a thick-and-thin pen, indicating the narrow sections by a filled-in area and the wider parts by lines, which will give a better impression of the finished lace (*see* diagram 11).

Dressing table set (Desirée)

This set is designed to demonstrate the development of a shape into a series of complementary designs. Commencing with the

Fig. 7. *Dressing Table Set in Schneeberg lace ('Desirée') – the same basic shapes have been developed in a different form for each item*

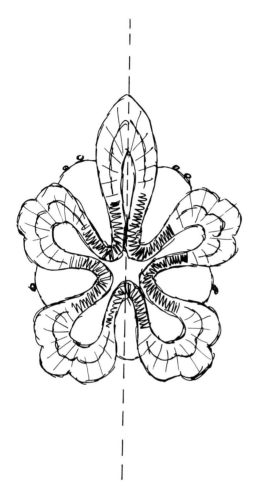

narrow whole stitch section. Strictly speaking, this design is not a pure Schneeberg pattern as the braid crosses itself, so it would be an excellent exercise to attempt a pure design using the same petal within the limitations of the narrow outline of a clothes brush. The outer plait of this pattern has picots and is carried across from one end to the other attaching itself only at the centre point.

Hair brush

Next in the series is the hair brush, The basic petal shape has been repeated four times and a leaf placed at one end to elongate the design,

Diag. 11. *Preliminary sketch for the Hair Brush pattern*

two basic shapes of a petal and a leaf, these patterns show that they can be so arranged in a different series and with only a slightly altered format to accommodate a variety of basic forms. Each piece of lace is worked using DMC Fil à Dentelle thread for workers and DMC Fil d'Or for passives.

Clothes brush

The first of the series is the clothes brush design (*see* pricking 7). This incorporates the petal shape at the ends, joined together with a

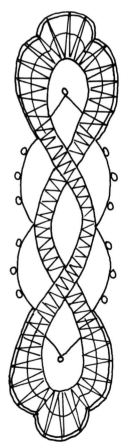

Pricking 7. *Clothes Brush design for Schneeberg dressing table set – 'Désirée'*

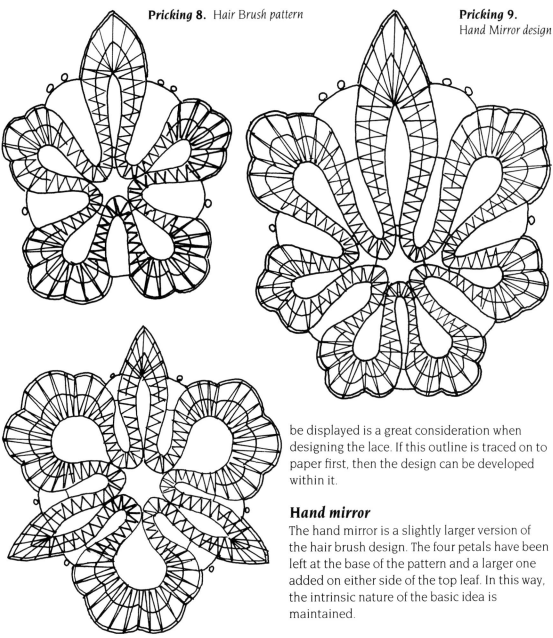

Pricking 8. *Hair Brush pattern*

Pricking 9.
Hand Mirror design

Pricking 10. *Pricking for Trinket Box Lace*

this making allowance for the shape of the brush itself. It must be remembered that the basic outline of the article in which the lace will

be displayed is a great consideration when designing the lace. If this outline is traced on to paper first, then the design can be developed within it.

Hand mirror

The hand mirror is a slightly larger version of the hair brush design. The four petals have been left at the base of the pattern and a larger one added on either side of the top leaf. In this way, the intrinsic nature of the basic idea is maintained.

Trinket box

Now comes the trinket box. This uses alternate petal and leaf shapes, which, in effect, produces a vaguely triangular shape which looks most attractive in a circular frame. The leaf points are made to protrude in order to break up the outline and add interest. If they were on a line with the petals, they would merge into the design and it could become rather montonous.

Round tray

The round tray design elaborates and enlarges the trinket box pattern and introduces another element which is basic to Schneeberg lace; the centre filling. This filling needs six pairs of bobbins. The work is commenced at the centre by making a plaited ring, and the ends are finished at the outside edge so that there are no ends within the work. Diagram 12 should be referred to in conjunction with the instructions that follow to work this filling.

Filling for centre of tray design: Hang on two pairs of bobbins at A and work a plait round the centre ring, putting in support pins to keep it in position. Sew in both pairs at the beginning to complete a circle. Twist both pairs four times and leave.

Hang on two pairs at X. Work a four-pair crossing (a windmill) with these and the two pairs from A. The pin is put in at B. Now take out pin X and slide the threads down to B. Plait these threads as far as D and leave. The two pairs left at B are each twisted six times more to be ready to join at C.

Hang on two pairs at Y and work a four-pair crossing with these and the two twisted pairs from B. Put in the pin at C and take out pin Y, sliding the threads down as before. Plait them

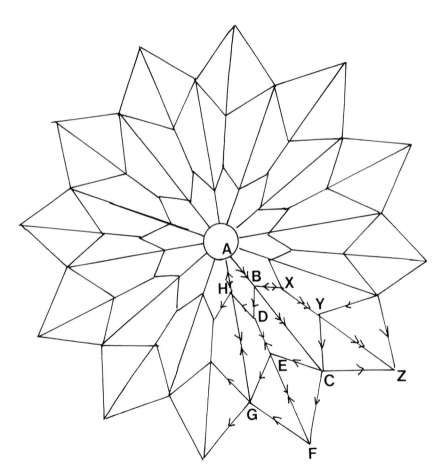

Diag. 12. *Working the centre of the tray design*

Pricking 11. Round Tray pattern (part of design)

as far as E. Plait the pairs which have come from A and sew both pairs into F. Now continue the plait with them as far as G and leave.

Put a support pin at D for the plait from B and, using the right-hand pair, twist it four times. Work a three-pair crossing with this pair and the plaited pairs from C. Put in pin E between the plaited pairs. Twist it six times more and work another three-pair crossing at E. (There is no need to use a second pin here.) Continue the plait towards G and leave. Twist the single pair from E four times and join it back with the pair left at D to plait as far as H, and leave.

Fig. 8. *'Pansy' – a simple motif in Schneeberg lace techniques*

Work a four-pair crossing with the plaits from F and E. Put in pin G and take the left-hand pair; twist it six times and work a three-pair crossing at H with this pair and the plaited pairs from D. Put in pin H between the plaited pairs. Twist the other pair four times; sew in to the plaited centre ring. Twist four times again and work another three-pair crossing with the pairs at H. Plait these pairs from H to the next point and leave. Twist the other pair six times and join it back in at G. Now work two plaits with the pairs at G to the next pin-hole.

Continue in this fashion until the starting point is reached. Now, following the arrows, work plaits and false plaits, where necessary, to finish with all the threads ready to sew in at Z. They are then finished in three bunches of four threads each as per the instructions for finishing the braids.

If these instructions have been a little confusing, the actual working is much easier,

but, of course, this area could always be substituted with a piece of material.

Pansy motif

Having experimented with a petal and a leaf, the next pricking, number 12, uses a single shape which repeats itself several times and allows the threads which are used to make the filling to be carried across the work rather than constantly finished and restarted. Eight pairs of bobbins are needed and, once again, DMC Fil à Dentelle thread is used. To design a motif in this manner, it is necessary to commence with a central point and draw radiating lines from this at equal angles. In this way, for four lines, the angle between them is 90° ; for five lines it is 72°; and for six lines it becomes 60° , and so on. Then one repeat of the design is drawn within two of the lines and this in turn is repeated by tracing it, so that each section is identical.

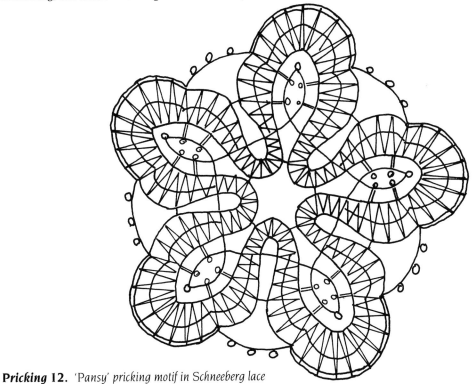

Pricking 12. *'Pansy' pricking motif in Schneeberg lace*

Bolero (*Fleur de Lys*)

This bolero motif (prickings 13*a* (far left) and 13*b* (left)) has been designed in an attempt to reproduce the effect of embossed material by overlaying it on a fabric lining. Rather than waste space by producing the pattern for the whole garment, it is better for any person wishing to work a similar one, to design their own basic garment shape thus making allowance for different sizes. The pattern is intended to be repetitive in the manner of an all-over wallpaper or fabric design. Each of the lines of motifs is staggered and interlocked with the adjacent ones. The outline of the next-door neighbours has been marked on the pricking of the motif as a guide. A simple edging pattern has also been included. The original piece of lace was made with BOUC 50 Fil de Lin thread and each motif worked separately, although joined to its neighbours with sewings.

Pricking 13. (a) '*Fleur de Lys*' *design for bolero (left)*
(b) *Edge pattern for bolero (above)*

Fig. 9. '*Fleur de Lys*' – *a Schneeberg lace bolero with an 'all-over' design*

Fig. 10. *'Orchid' – a Schneeberg lace fan made in lemon and gold*

The fan (Orchid)

The final design is a fan called 'Orchid' (*see* pricking 14). Once again, only one section has been included to encourage the lacemaker's understanding of this type of lace when assembling the sections in order to make the entire fan. The orchid flower is growing at the top of a stem with large leaves sprouting below. The filling stitch of tallies follows through the leaf theme, with a plaited stem and leaves uniting the sections to strengthen the lace at every other fan stick. Six complete repeats of pattern will be required, but, if preferred, the design can be made into a mat edging using twelve complete repeats of pattern. The fillings for this design can be carried across the back of the work in most cases.

Pricking 14. *'Orchid' – a fan design in Schneeberg lace (six repeats of pattern needed for whole fan)*

5 · Designing crosses

A cross can be defined as a pair of straight lines which pass through one another, usually forming a right angle at this crossing point. Crosses can be found in a variety of forms. Diagram 13 shows some of them. 13a represents a Greek cross. In 13b the arms have been rotated through 45° to form the cross of St. Andrew. 13c has an elongated lower arm and is used mainly as the symbol of the Christian faith. 13d is usually known as the Celtic cross and incorporates a ring which is generally regarded to represent a halo or nimbus. The Maltese cross (13e) is based on the cross of St Andrew but the shape is formed by the space between the arms becoming solid with a blank area representing the line of the cross. In lace designs, this last shape of cross is normally only depicted as one single element within a larger piece of work and is a significant feature of Maltese lace patterns. Designs using the other crosses can be easily made once the symmetry

and proportions of them are understood and the method of working the pattern is learned.

Torchon crosses

The most conventional and traditional of the shapes used in lacemaking is the Christian cross. As this incorporates the necessary geometry needed to work any of the other cross shapes as well, let us concentrate on this one and imagine a design to be made for Torchon lace. By referring to diagram 14 and using graph paper, commence by drawing the two centre lines which pass across one another at A. These

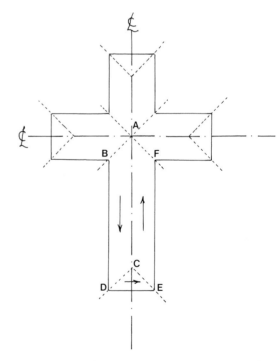

Diag. 14. *Working diagram for designing and making Torchon lace crosses*

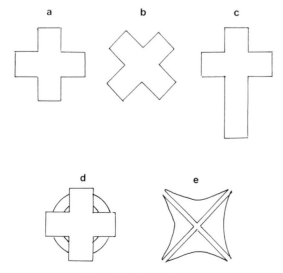

Diag. 13. *Types of crosses*

◆

must be at right angles to one another. The basic square shape can then be drawn around these axes making sure that the width of each arm remains constant and is equidistant on either side of the centre lines. The use of graph paper assists in obtaining this symmetry without recourse to complicated measuring procedures. The method of working the cross must now be considered before going any further.

If the lace were to be worked commencing at the top and finishing at the bottom, a large number of extra bobbins would be required to work the side arms. This would cause the problem of discarding all the extra threads which would either form a fringe hanging from these arms or would produce a rather bulky edge finish. Neither of these would make an attractive piece of work. So, having rejected this method of working, we must have a second look at the basic shape. Starting at any point on the edge, a continuous line can be drawn all the way round until the starting point is reached. So it seems logical to consider working the lace itself that way and all the thread ends can be sewn into their commencement places.

Extending this reasoning, and remembering that the original two lines are the skeleton of the design, this edge line can be widened inwards to cover the entire area of the cross up to the centre line, and it will still be possible to use it as a continuous line, turning the corners as it travels round the shape. Now, having discovered that corners are required, start at the centre point A and draw straight lines from here to each of the inner corners of the arms. Immediately two lines at 45° to the vertical and horizontal arms are formed. Knowing that Torchon lace uses this angle for its design, the solution is obvious. The lace must be worked down one side, up the other and so on round the entire shape.

To discover where the other corners are within the shape, add more diagonal lines thus:

starting at each of the corner points of the arms, draw a line as far as the centre line. You will notice that a triangle, which is in reality a quarter of a square, has been formed at the end of each arm. These diagonal lines can be used as if they were the corners of a mat or edging. So the work can be commenced on diagonal AB and carried down to CD. The pillow is turned through 90° to work across to CE and then again through another 90° to work up to AF, and so on. The threads at the centre on line AC are twisted three or four times and passed round the pins and sewings are made along it, in order to join it all together and to give a neat appearance to the work.

It is very important to ensure that the ratio of the width to the length of each arm is correct. If the width is too great, a thick and heavy shape is formed; if too thin, the finished cross appears anorexic and is very spindly. In the same way, the ratio of the length of the three shorter arms to the lower central stem must be correct. This longer central leg must be at least twice (or even a little more than) the length of each arm to make the correctly balanced shape. If it is any shorter, it gives the impression that, perhaps, the designer has made an error and had originally intended it to be the same length as the others.

Now, having explored the geometry and the working methods of Torchon crosses, it should be possible to design a pattern that will fit all these criteria. The Torchon cross design (pricking 15) has been made using the above principles and is worked in BOUC 120 Fil de Lin using eleven pairs of bobbins.

Braid lace crosses

When it comes to designing a 'free' or braid lace cross, a slightly different method is required. A rough sketch of the intended shape is, of course, necessary in order to get a general impression of the finished lace. This should

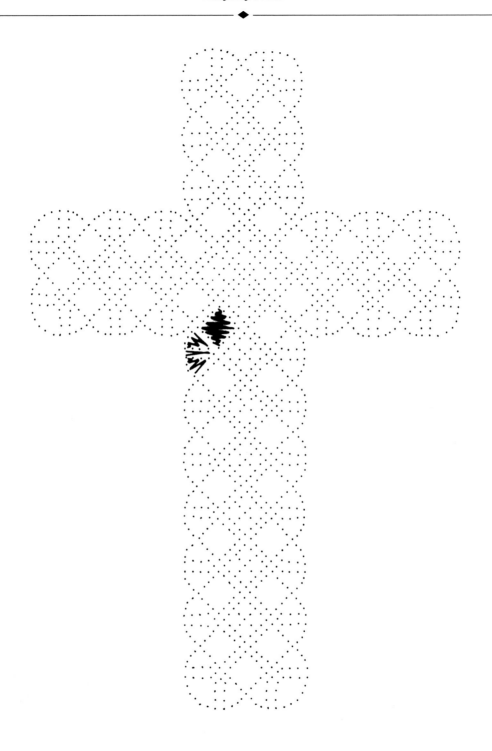

Pricking 15. *Torchon cross*

always be an automatic first step for any design. When translating this sketch into the actual pricking, the first step, as before, is to draw the two axes. Remember that the lace on either side of each axis is a mirror image of itself. To achieve this, trace the half that is already drawn. Now reverse the tracing paper and trace the same shape again but on the other side of the centre line, checking that the side arms as well as the upright arms are reflecting one another about their axis. If only one small deviation to this symmetry is made, the finished lace has a lop-sided appearance, so it is worthwhile spending a little more time at this point to obtain true symmetry. It must also be remembered that the longer stem of the cross is an elongated version of the shorter three arms. Therefore, to make it compatible with them, any filling needed will require adjustment accordingly.

Bruges Flower Work cross

Pricking 16 has been developed in the style of Bruges Flower Work on the above principle. The design is worked in BOUC 80 Fil de Lin with 14 pairs of bobbins for the flower and 6 pairs for the braids. The central point becomes the centre of a flower and each arm is a braid ending in scrolls. Every part of the design must now be linked in some way. Taking the idea of a corona as found in the Celtic crosses, each of these separate elements is joined together by a circle into a unified whole. The space within this ring could be left blank but if some type of filling stitch is required, the lines of this must be continuous throughout. To ensure this, it is best to draw in the working lines lightly across the whole area and then erase any parts that are to be hidden by the flower. If the braid circle were to be drawn larger so that it joined the arms further away from the central point, the arms would not stand out as clearly as they do

Fig. 11. *A Torchon cross*

Fig. 12. *Cross in Bruges Flower Work*

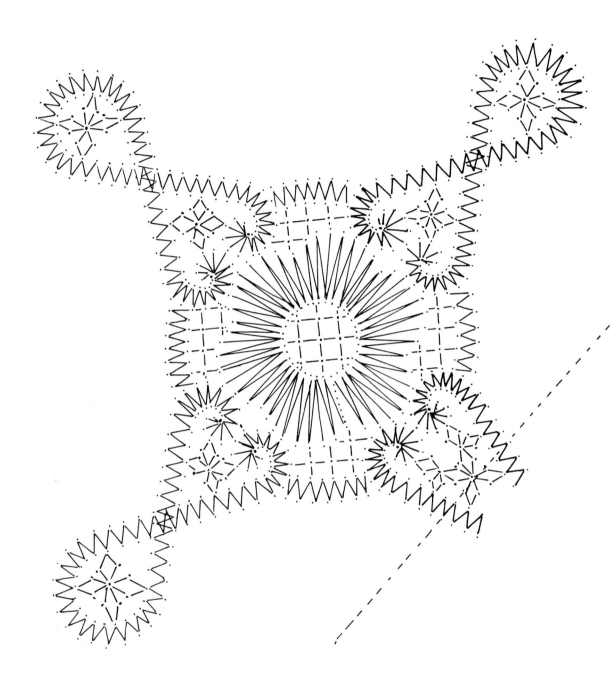

Pricking 16. Bruges Flower Work Cross design (*top*)

and the overall effect of the cross shape would disappear. Once again, note the extra length of the stem. At this juncture, practise drawing various shapes in order to see the different effect of these proportions.

Gold cross

The third cross (pricking 17, overleaf) is a very simple shape based on the 'onion' domes found on religious buildings in countries bordering the shores of the Mediterranean Sea and further east. This design demonstrates the absolute

Fig. 13. *'Onion Dome' – a cross worked in gold thread*

need for perfect symmetry about each centre line. A slight deviation on any one of the curved lines would completely distort the final shape. To work this pattern, the braid edge requires five pairs of bobbins wound with DMC Fil d'Or, and the worker pair uses DMC Fil a Dentelle no. 744 in yellow. The tally filling requires four pairs of bobbins wound with the same gold thread.

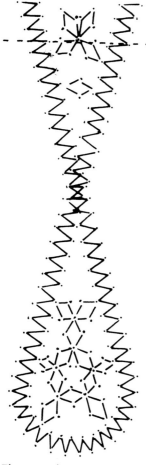

Bruges Flower Work Cross design (bottom)

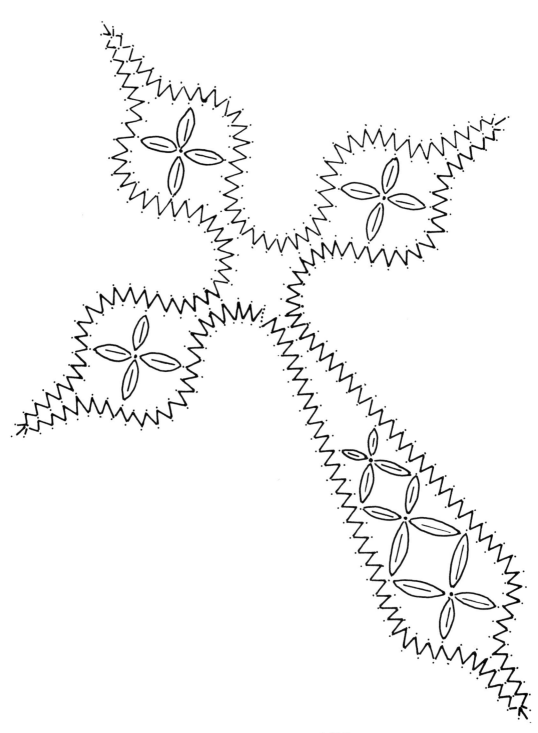

Pricking 17. 'Onion Dome' Gold Cross

6 · The importance of line and space

A design consists of a number of lines with space in between them. The quality of these lines and the ratio of their width to this space is all important. Straight lines can be drawn on a piece of paper in such a way that they will produce an optical illusion of depth where, in reality, there is none. According to its position, an object can appear either to stand out or to recede into the distance. There are any number of well-known illusions which illustrate this phenomenon.

When making a design for a piece of lace, various types of line are required. The first lines drawn will produce a silhouette. This is the basic shape of the finished work. Whether the type of lace is to be traditional or modern, this will always apply. The structural lines are usually the next to appear. These are the main dividing lines within the silhouette. For example: if the main outline is a leaf, the veins will be the structural lines; if a house, they will be the doors and windows. And finally, the detail lines are drawn to produce any background required and to demonstrate the position of any shading or texture that will be needed. By the time this stage is reached, the space within the silhouette lines will be determined and any area required to be left blank will not need any shading lines.

A line is not just a straight narrow mark made with pen or pencil on a piece of paper. It can be made into something animated. Vertical lines can be drawn to denote architectural quality and to give the appearance of height to an object. Horizontal ones usually represent the scenic qualities of calmness and security. Lines can be given movement which may denote rhythm or moods and feelings such as temper or elation. The character given to a line is formed by the amount of curve that is put on it. A completely straight line gives the impression of speed and directness, whilst a wavy line, especially if it crosses over itself, produces a wandering, devious effect. Think of the straight lines formed by the speed of water coming down a waterfall and how the same water becomes slow and lethargic as it meanders lazily in large loops across the plain. Large curves depict slowness and lethargy but a tightly spiralled line can appear busy and fussy. Circular lines and spirals are also used to direct the eye towards a central focal point whilst radiating straight lines open up a centre, as the opening bud of a flower reveals the inside of the petals.

It is worthwhile practising drawing a simple scene several times using lines of varying curves and angles, to develop an awareness of how they can change the mood of a design. If, for example, we return to the waterfall mentioned above, we need straight vertical lines for the drop of water to indicate the speed and rush of the falling liquid, and circular lines at the base to depict the swirl of the foaming water there.

Another exercise can be worked using a piece of thin string or thick thread. Drop it on to a piece of paper and mark the outline in pencil. Now pull and push various parts of it into other shapes and note the difference in feeling that is obtained and the infinite variety of shapes which can be obtained from this single line.

The relationship between a line, whether

straight or curved, and the space around it, is very important when producing a design. Within any shape, there must be areas left either completely void of thread or with very open stitches in order to allow the main lines to predominate. If an outline is allowed to become submerged in a mass of fancy stitchery, its importance becomes lost and the onlooker's eye is drawn to the lesser sections instead of the main feature. This is more vital if the work is all one colour, than if different colours are used for the various elements in the design, although

even then, if the wrong colours are chosen for the fillings, they can dominate the outline which they should be complementing.

Width of lines

The width of a line equals the space between two drawn lines of pattern, between which will be worked a braid of lace producing a single line on the finished piece of work. Therefore, two single lines of pricking produce one single line of a certain width. Although the space

Diag. 15. *Comparison of braid widths*

surrounding a line is of major concern, the width of the line itself is of equal importance for a braid lace. When the design is drawn, the outline of the shapes will normally be the first lines to appear. Then secondary lines inside the basic shapes are denoted to give strength to the outline. It is the relationship between these two lines and the size of the basic shape which must be in proportion to attain the maximum effect. If the distance between them is too small, when this area is worked the outline will be thin and insubstantial, but if it is too great a heavy thick shape emerges (*see* diagram 15). It is not possible to state exactly what the distances

between these two lines should be. The actual size of the drawing and the thread to be used must be taken into consideration, as must the relationship between that part of the overall design and the rest of it.

Referring back to the tree in diagram 15, if the outline were to remain as in (*a*), and there were to be no filling stitches, when the lace were taken off the pillow, it would distort and twist. It should not be substantial enough to hold its shape. Conversely, in (*b*), the braid is far too thick and chunky and it would be very difficult to work it evenly. Whereas in (*c*) the ratio is correct and the outline is strong enough to be

Fig. 14. *'Tea Pot' motif — intended for use on a tea cosy*

bold, yet fine enough to give the lace a delicate appearance. It would hold its shape better and yet not appear too heavy even if there were no filling stitches.

Teapot design

The Teapot design (pricking 18) demonstrates this correct ratio. It is worked in BOUC 80 Fil de Lin and ten pairs of bobbins are required. The horizontal lines are curved to give the impression of a three-dimensional object rather

than a cross-section of one. The lid has been given different treatment to the main part because it is a separate entity although an integral part of the whole piece. The internal measurements of the pot are too great to use one single filling stitch in this area. It requires a focal point to attract the eye and yet must still allow the main outline to dominate. Any number of simple motifs could be inserted here instead of the single word 'tea' but they must have a link with the object itself and must be attached to the outline braid in some way. The use of radiating lines draws the eye towards this focal point and right through the pattern whilst

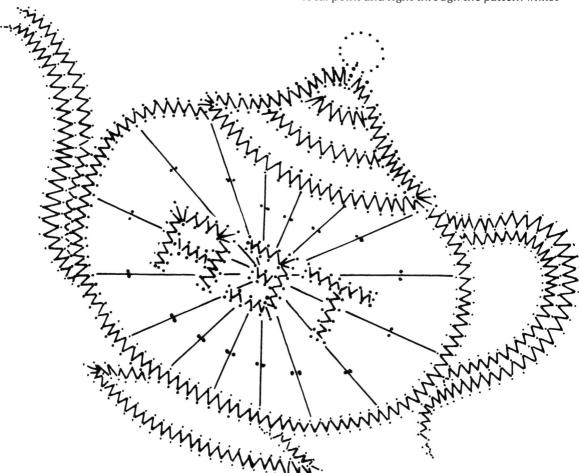

Pricking 18. *'Tea Pot' motif*

retaining the importance of the main shape. When making a design of one motif within another, do not attach the inner one to the outer at too many places. It is far better to understate than to overstate a point and the main intention will stand out far more clearly this way.

Sky at Night motif

The relationship of one object to another in size and position is investigated in pricking 19 (The Sky at Night). This design has been made with the intention of using it in a ring and suspending it to hang freely. It is worked using Gütermann silver thread with DMC Brillante

Fig. 15. *'Sky at Night' – a simple motif worked in silver and white threads*

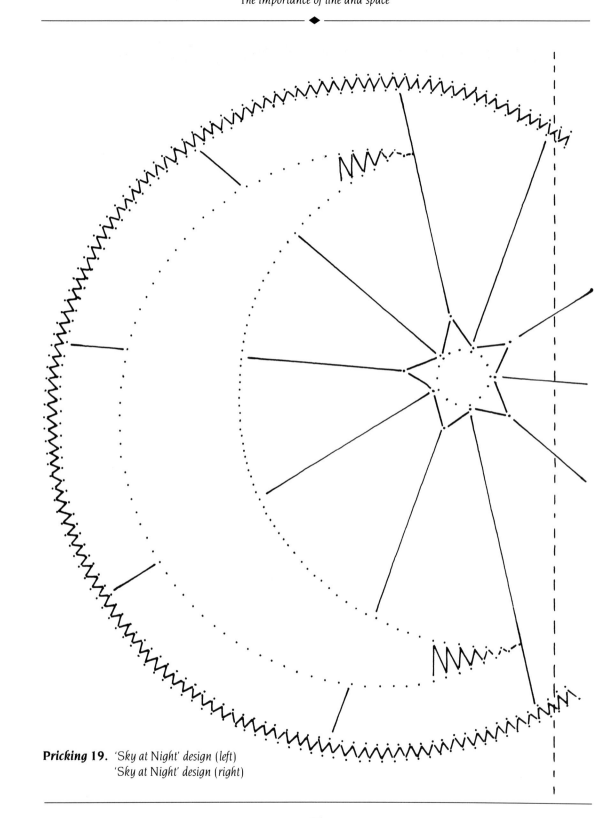

Pricking 19. *'Sky at Night' design* (left)
'Sky at Night' design (right)

d'Alsace 30 in white. The white thread is used as the worker pair for the outer ring and as twisted passive pairs at each edge of the moon. If the silver thread were used on its own, the lace would not lie flat. The outer ring completely encloses a space and yet that inner area is intended to represent infinity. As much of it as possible has been left blank so that the eye can see some distance through it.

When drawing a crescent moon, the radius of the inner line is slightly less than that for the outer edge and the centre point is moved. The silver threads are used so that when light shines on it there is a 'twinkle' which resembles that seen when looking at the real moon. The star must be in proportion to the moon and not too large or too near it, in order to add some realism to the design. It would be wrong, in this case, to work a braid outline with a filling for the moon shape. For one thing, the stitches would be squashed up together, and for another, the finished lace would be far too open. Half-stitch is extremely useful when working curved shapes. The working lines of the lace itself take on a curved appearance and follow the shape of the basic outline and yet the threads are close enough together to give the impression of solidity. In this design, the use of space is very clear. Although the moon, star and outer frame are connected with plaits, there are only enough to hold the work together. The lines of the star points have a dual purpose being extended to form an integrated whole and positioned so that the ends of the moon are attached. As an exercise, practise putting the star in different positions in relation to the moon and notice how the whole effect is altered.

Lines and circles

At this point, another property of a line can be explored. If the two ends of a line are joined together, a continuous circular shape is formed. The spaces on either side of the original line

Bruges Flower Work mat

will still exist but, whereas one of them reaches to infinity, the other is now an enclosed, finite area. The line itself can take on any number of forms with either straight or curved sections, or both. As a circle, it is still only one continuous line, but if it is stretched at a number of different places, it can take on a variety of shapes. Circles, ovals, triangles, squares, hexagons, octogons, etc. are a few of the regular shapes, but any number of irregular shapes can be formed. The list is endless. Using a piece of thread as before, join the two ends and experiment with making different shapes. Once sharp angles are made at different places on this line, its character is completely altered. The lazy meanders formed by the curved lines are transformed into a busy, direct shape which appears to be divided into several sections, although there is still only one line. When designing a piece of lace, these differences must be taken into account. It is possible to combine these effects to produce an attractive piece of lace. Many filling stitches are made of straight lines although they can frequently give the illusion of curves as in the half stitch moon on pricking 19. Bruges Flower Work is a very suitable lace for demonstrating these possibilities.

If we refer to diagram 16 and draw a circle, the basic outside shape is formed (16*a*). If this circle is indented at six equidistant places, a six-sided petalled shape has been formed (16*b*). A ring has become a flower! Now twist the line so that loops are formed at the indentations where the petals join (16*c*). The shape still consists of one single line but there are six small spaces formed within the large inner space. If a second continuous line is drawn with straight sections touching the places where these loops come towards the centre of the inner space, a hexagon appears (16*d*) which effectively creates six more spaces. A large flower has now been formed which needs filling stitches in its petals to bring them to the fore. To follow the basic flower shape throughout the design, repeat it in a smaller form in each of the large spaces, and pricking 20 (overleaf) appears. Now we have six small flowers within one large one. The main filling stitch is hexagonal to reiterate the shape of the inner basic line so that it also has a link throughout the pattern. In this way, a design can be formed whose continuity is maintained by using the principle of a line with its two ends joined together.

The pattern which evolved in this manner uses BOUC 50 Fil de Lin thread. The braids and inner ring of the flowers require 7 pairs of bobbins and the petals need 11 pairs.

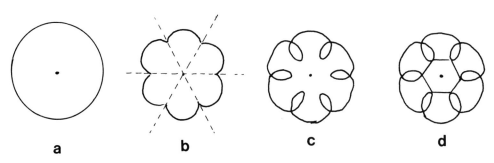

a **b** **c** **d**

Diag. 16. *Converting a line into a circle, loops and hexagonal flower*

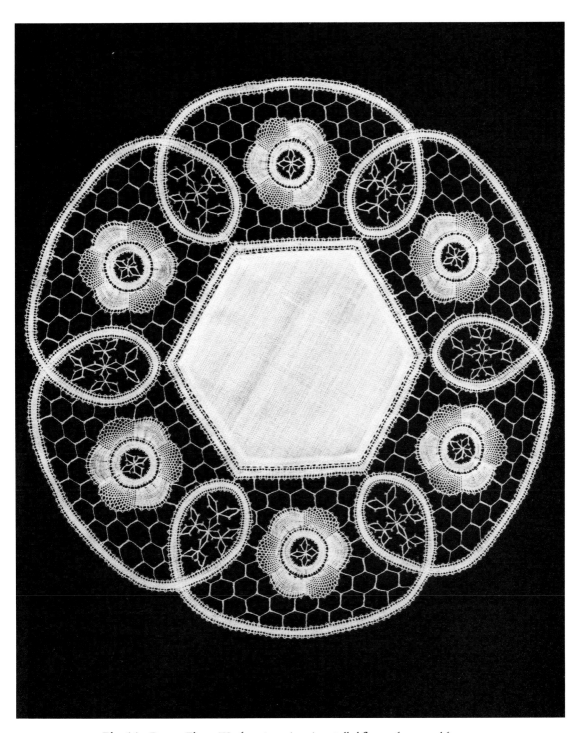

Fig. 16. Bruges Flower Work mat – using six-petalled flower shapes and hexagons

Pricking 20. Bruges Flower Work design for mat edging (six repeats needed)

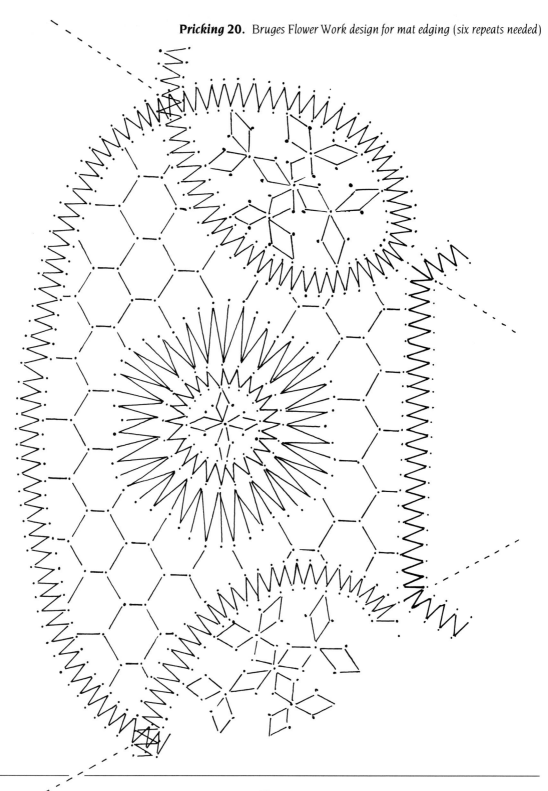

7 · Using Metallized threads

Making lace with metal thread is not new. Many of the very first laces made during the sixteenth century and before were constructed with a silver or gold thread. Unfortunately, the majority of these pieces of work have not survived. This is partly due to the fact that the value of the thread was so high that, when a piece of lace became redundant or out of fashion, it was unpicked and remade into a fresh piece. Also, the metal became tarnished very easily and thus the work was not appreciated when it became a dirty grey colour rather than having the brilliant sparkling effect it had when newly made. It must also be presumed that much of this lace was smelted down to make other objects, when it became unfashionable, and some of it would have been buried with its owner. The fashion for gold and silver lace did not last, however, and it became primarily the province of the Church; eventually only ecclesiastical metallic lace was made and used.

According to Emily Reigate in her book *The Illustrated Guide to Lace*, in spite of the fact that gold and silver threads were still being made into lace for Court wear in the late sixteenth and seventeenth centuries, most lace for other purposes was made using linen or silk thread by this time, although Genoa was still famous for its metallic laces.

During the last two decades of the eighteenth century, a fashion arose to remove the gold and silver from old lace thread. A machine was invented which separated them so that the metal fell into one box and the rest of the thread into another. In this way, while this fashion was in vogue, the remaining gold and silver laces and braids of Europe were almost entirely destroyed.

Modern metallic threads

Gold, silver and other coloured threads are now becoming popular amongst lacemakers in the late twentieth century. These modern versions are not made from the actual metal but are synthetic and need very careful treatment. A DMC thread has been available for some years which has a cotton core with gold or silver wrapped around it. The finished thread is very smooth in appearance but it has a nasty habit of cracking to reveal the inner core during use. It is very difficult when winding the bobbins to prevent this cracking, and it is virtually impossible to work a sewing without the metal surface peeling away. This thread has now been superseded by a far superior version which is a three-core twisted thread, each strand of which can be separated to form a much finer thread if required. Each element of the thread has a man-made fibre as a core with a metal coating, a process which has eliminated the cracking. It is not a smooth thread, however, but the rough surface produces a more glittery effect when a light is shone on it.

MEZ also produce a very good range of metallic and polyester threads called Effektgarn. These do not readily separate like the DMC ones and the surface is very rough, but it gives an excellent finish to the work. Gütermann metallic threads are made in a variety of lovely colours in addition to the traditional gold and silver. Once again, these have a polyester core and the metallic filaments are twisted round this. They do separate if care is not taken but the finished lace is firm and attractive. The Madeira company makes a large range of metallized threads suitable for lacemaking, as well as a number of other crafts including machine embroidery. They are available in a comprehensive range of colours and produce good lace when used correctly and mixed with cotton or linen threads.

It is not always advisable to make lace with a thread primarily intended for use as an embroidery thread, or one meant to be used on a sewing machine. I have found that these threads do not always hold their shape when worked in bobbin lace. They are often too soft and the lace tends to curl up when taken off the pillow. Even worked in conjunction with cotton or linen threads, they are not entirely satisfactory. Conversely, threads intended for

use by lacemakers are not always suitable for embroidery, especially cross stitch work. A sample should always be worked before commencing any piece of work to avoid future disappointment.

So it can be seen that there are a far greater number of metallic threads available for the modern lacemaker to use than there has been in the past, and an increasingly greater variety is being manufactured each year which makes it impossible to name them all. The only way one can possibly know which of them will produce good lace is to use them and experiment with as many as possible.

Fig. 17. *'Gold Swan' – a picture using different thicknesses of gold thread*

Metallic thread handicaps

There are other problems attached to the use of this type of thread which do not arise when using natural fibres. Most of these problems arise in the physical use of them. For example, the slip knot used to prevent threads from unwinding on the bobbins provides hours of innocent fun when using a metallized thread! Most of these threads have a will of their own and either refuse to allow the slip knot to stay in place or, conversely, will not allow it to unwind when necessary, permitting instead the rest of the thread to unravel, whilst the actual knot stays firmly in place. This seems to be a universal hazard when using these metallized threads. If anyone has a secret method of use which is infallible, please let me know!

Another complication arises predominantly when working sectional laces. When attempting to work a sewing with many metallized threads, they tend to disintegrate. They have a nasty habit of splitting so that only a part of the thread is drawn through the loop, or they break altogether leaving short ends. This dilemma can partly be eliminated in the solving of yet another predicament. When working a braid in metal threads, the passives become difficult to pull tightly into position and the finished work has a corrugated effect. Both problems can be eliminated if the worker pair of the braid is a linen or cotton thread of the same colour as the metal thread, or is white if using a silver thread. When working a metallic filling inside a braid outline, the loops formed by the pins and worker threads, being of cotton or linen material, easily allow the metal filling thread to be drawn through smoothly as there are no rough edges against which it might be snagged. The use of this other thread is virtually undetectable in the finished lace, and when straightening the passive threads to form an even fabric, they move into position easily, sliding against the smooth worker threads.

When using a yellow cotton worker pair together with a gold metallized passive thread, the depth of colour can be changed. A darker tone of yellow will produce a finished piece which is a lovely rich, dark golden colour; whilst a pale yellow thread results in a delicate, light gold piece of lace. Variegated thread, when used as a worker, must be wound so that both bobbins will have thread of the same tone at the same time. When a thread of this type is used in this context the finished work produces a variety of depth of colour which is most attractive. This method of working with different threads cannot be used when making a braid in half stitch, however. It can only be used in whole stitch braids because, in half stitch, only one thread of a pair travels across the braid and the other one becomes a passive. This produces a peculiar tartan effect with only one odd cotton thread weaving amongst all the metallic ones.

When designing for lace to be made with metallic threads, with or without the assistance of cotton or linen threads, it must be remembered that the metallizing process produces a stiffer thread so that any stitches used will not produce as soft an effect as threads made from natural fibres. When viewed under a magnifying glass, the outline of the metal thread is somewhat irregular and angular instead of having a smooth rounded appearance. This means that any filling stitches must be kept simple in order to prevent an untidy, cluttered look.

Gold Swan

The Gold Swan (pricking 21) has been worked with this in mind. The swans of Bruges inspired this shape which was originally drawn with the intention of working it as a tape lace with needle-made fillings. The outline was sketched in roughly and then smoothed using French curves. It is important to get the complete outline in proportion for this type of motif, and to ensure that the points of the tail and wing follow the line of a smooth curve in order that their relationship is correct. If this is not done, the design does not flow from one section to another. Here also, is the ideal opportunity to demonstrate the need for blank spaces within the design to emphasise the gaps between neck and wing, and wing and tail sections. At first glance, the design appears to be made using only one type of gold thread, but in reality three different types of thread are used. The braid outline is made using the principle of working with only the passives in metallic thread and the workers in cotton thread. These passives used DMC Fil d'Or a Broder and the worker pair DMC Brillante d'Alsace 30 in yellow. This combination of threads gives a good firm edging, but when the filling stitches are considered, a softer, more fluid thread is required and the DMC thread is a little too tough and thick to obtain the required effect. So the filling uses a finer Madeira metallized thread of the same gold colour.

Pricking 21. *'Gold Swan'*

In order to attempt to reproduce the texture of a swan, the fillings must give the impression of the feathers, and the line of lie of these (as on all birds) must be taken into consideration. The triangular ground is ideal for this purpose but it is worthwhile experimenting with other fillings to see if a better effect could be achieved by using a different stitch.

Candle design

The Christmas card Candle design (pricking 22) is, once again, simple in conception, but could be made more elaborate by incorporating this motif within a larger design. When drawing candles, do not make them too regimented. It is better not to have them all sitting on the same line or to have them exactly the same size. A little variety is necessary to stop the finished design becoming monotonous and dull. Interest is given here by using a variegated Madeira metallized thread for the filling stitches whilst the outside braid edge is worked with Gütermann gold metallic passive threads and DMC Brillante d'Alsace 30 pale yellow for the workers. Within each candle, the filling stitches are also slightly different from one another.

Bells

Pricking 23 shows yet another refinement. The three bell shapes were traced from a Christmas card picture which incorporated them within

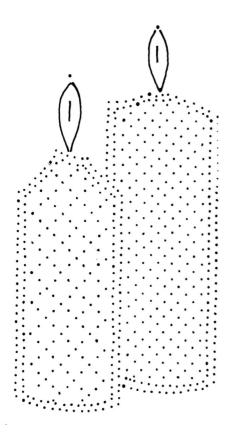

Pricking 22. *'Candles', design for a Christmas card*

Fig. 18. *'Two Candles' – a Christmas card design in gold threads*

another design, but the bow was drawn free-hand. By using silver passive threads and white workers for the outline, a strong shape emerges. The filling stitches, as for the candles, are worked in a variegated Madeira thread. Once again, by making sure that each bell has different stitches, they are given individuality and yet each of them produces a similar density of thread. The bow is worked in DMC Brillante d'Alsace 30, picking out one of the colours of the variegated fillings, and is worked in half stitch and ten-stick.

When drawing bells, care must be taken to give the flat design an impression of roundness.

Fig. 19. *'Three Bells' – a Christmas card worked in silver with a turquoise bow*

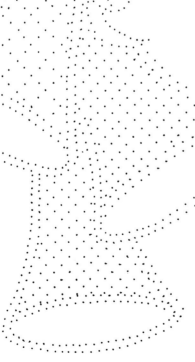

Pricking 23. *'Bells', a design for a Christmas card*

Fig. 20. *'Snowflake' – a motif in silver and white, mounted in a craft ring to create a 'Ramhanger'*

Pricking 24. *'Snowflake' pattern to use as a 'Ramhanger' (part of pricking)*

◆

This frequently means that part of the inside is depicted. This inner part becomes as important as the outside. Because it is not usually a visible part, and is the back, so to speak, it must be darker than the front outside part. This contrast is best depicted when using a very dark background material when mounting the work. Note the use of faceted sequins to represent the clappers. These catch the light reflecting the silver outline and also give continuity of line downwards throughout the design.

Snowflake 'Ramhanger'

Up to this point we have only considered using a cotton or linen thread as an invisible tool to give a better finish to work when using metallic threads. They can also be used in designs where both have equal importance and lay side by side in the completed piece of work. The Snowflake (pricking 24) is a good example of how this can be achieved. The base for this type of design is a craft ring, sometimes known as a lampshade ring, which can be purchased at most craft shops. These rings are usually made of metal and must be covered with either tape or thread before use. This one is covered with a crocheted edge in one of the same silver threads that is used to make the lace.

When designing circular patterns it is difficult to choose a suitable thread that will be correct for the central parts as well as the outer sections. This problem is also found when designing fans and circular mats. One method

of overcoming it is to design the pattern in more than one circular section so that allowance is made for the change in distance between the pin-holes. The same thread can be used, but there are fewer pattern repeats in the centre section.

Another method is to use different thicknesses of thread in conjunction with fewer repeats in each section. The effect of doing this is demonstrated here, and four different threads are used. The outer star shape is worked using Twilley's 'Goldfingering' silver thread for the worker and outer passive pairs of the Torchon shell, and BOUC Fil de Lin 50 in white for the rest. The inner section is worked using Gütermann silver thread for the equivalent parts and white BOUC Fil de Lin 100 to complement it.

When designing this type of pattern, polar graph paper is needed, and you must make sure that the sections into which it is divided are equal. Draw the ring shape on the graph paper first, so that the exact size of the finished design is known. Then divide this circle into equal radiating sections (in this case twelve). Now the basic finished outline shape can be sketched in, followed by the working lines and pin-hole positions. The centre section has only six repeats of pattern, thus attaching itself to the outer part at every other repeat only. Place the crochet-covered ring on the pillow whilst making the lace and work sewings over the edge with the silver worker pair at each point where the snowflake and ring touch.

8 · Animals in lace

Laces of all types have always included representations of animals and birds within many of their designs. Pat Earnshaw, in her book *Lace in Fashion*, includes a picture of a cutwork pattern published in 1587 which incorporates birds and animals in the design. She describes this as typical of the late Elizabethan and Jacobean periods. So those of us who may imagine that we have invented a new lace form must realize that there is nothing new under the sun. All that we are attempting is a different approach to a traditional theme.

Animals and birds can be some of the most complicated of designs to work. Even if an outline braid is all that is required, frequently it cannot be worked in one single piece. When extra detail is needed in the finished piece of work, the actual construction can become very intricate and is not always recommended for a novice lacemaker. You have only to look at some of the beautiful laces incorporating animals that were designed by the Bedford lace merchant, Thomas Lester, in the nineteenth century, to realize the complexity of some of their structure. However, it is worthwhile investigating some of the procedures for designing and working similar shapes.

Animals can be represented in lace in any number of different ways. A straightforward shape can be worked or a silhouette may be made. Likewise, a pattern can be a braid outline with fillings, or each section may be worked in its entirety with no separate outline. Alternatively, the creature may be a single motif or part of a more intricate design. The actual animal may be represented as a photograph or it may be stylized. The threads used can be either all white or monochrome, or they may even be glorious technicolour. The variations are inexhaustible and the choice is yours.

In the same way, the sources of inspiration are many and varied. For those of us who will never be a Stubbs or a Renoir, there are illustrations in books, photographs, embroidery transfers, greetings cards etc. to use as starting points for designs. If we commence by making a pricking for a simple animal outline motif, this can act as a basis for development into more complex patterns.

Arabian camel

The Arabian camel (pricking 25) can be used to illustrate the working techniques for this. It can be worked in DMC Brillante d'Alsace 30 or BOUC 120 Fil de Lin and requires up to five pairs of bobbins. The original picture upon which this design is based can be found in a 'Ladybird' book on African mammals. It is a small picture but very clear in detail. The first step when using such a picture is to draw or trace the outline of the animal. At this point, the required size of the finished piece of lace must be determined and, if necessary, the outline adjusted accordingly, either by enlargement or reduction using squared paper, or by resorting to the nearest photocopying machine! In either case, the correctly sized outline will need to be retraced on to another piece of tracing paper in order to prepare the final pricking. This second tracing is required because the outline must be worked face down as the lace is always worked wrong side up and none of us has X-ray eyes!

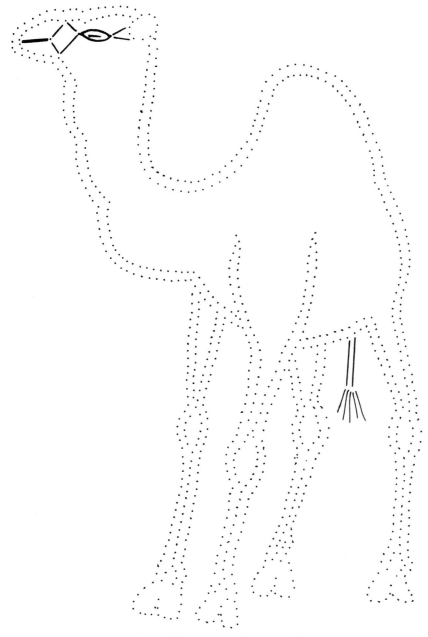

Pricking 25. 'Arabian Camel'

Fig. 21. *'Arabian Camel' – note the picots on its hump. The hooves and ears are worked in ten-stick which provides a change of texture to the outline without adding more threads*

Thread choice

If you have not already done so, before continuing further, you must give consideration to the thread or threads that will be required to work the animal. Try to keep the thread as fine as is practical for the size of the finished lace. A more attractive piece of work will be produced by using a fine thread which needs more passive pairs and closer pin-holes than if a thicker thread is used, which would make the braid coarser. This is also preferable when using coloured threads because a much greater range of colours is available for the finer threads than the thicker ones. The background material on which the motif is to be mounted will also have a bearing on the texture of the thread to be

used. If the mount is to be a coarse hessian or linen material, then it is better to use that type of thread to make the lace. A piece of work made with shiny, fine silk thread would look incongruous on a rough, loosely woven material. Likewise, the colour of the mount must complement that of the motif so that it enhances but does not swamp it, nor allows the motif to disappear into the background.

Drawing the outline braid

Once a satisfactorily sized basic shape is ready and the threads and background material decided upon, check again to ensure that any undesirable bumps are ironed out and that the outline is a smooth line without losing its essential shape and appearance. To make this outline into a simple braid pattern, a second line is needed which is drawn inside the basic shape. The distance between these two lines must be compatible with the overall size and reference should be made to the instructions in the section on 'Line and space' in order to achieve this. It should also remain constant throughout the pattern except for, perhaps, the legs and ears. There are occasions when it is desirable to have a varying width of outline braid, but this particular exercise is meant to be a first attempt and not an advanced piece of work.

When beginning to draw the second line, it is necessary first to determine which part of the animal would be nearest to you if it were a solid creature and not a flat drawing. This is usually some part of the head (ears or nose perhaps) but it could be one of the haunches or shoulders. Commence drawing the inner line at point and follow round each of the sections as they become further away. Use a ruler to mark the required distance between the lines. Do not attempt to mark it by eye until you have had a lot of practice. Measure it at frequent intervals and then join up these marks to make the inner lines. Diagram 17 shows the effects obtained on

◆

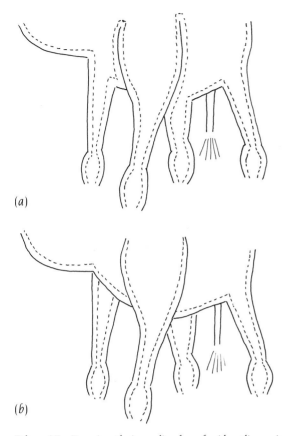

(a)

(b)

Diag. 17. *Drawing the inner line for a braid outline animal*
(a) incorrect   (b) correct

the under body and top legs of the camel with the second line drawn correctly and wrongly. Do not follow the outline blindly in one piece unless the work is to be used as a silhouette only, with no internal markings at all. This produces an unrealistic effect as can be seen in the diagram. Nor is it necessary to put a second line on any part of the animal which is behind a section already drawn. This produces a thick section as shown in diagram 17*a* and an animal which is anatomically incorrect. Diagram 17*b* shows the right method of marking the second inner line so that a true representation of the animal is made.

Completing the Pattern

Once the braid's inner line has been drawn, lightly mark the pin-hole positions on the outside curves following the instructions in the section on 'Braid lace design'. The complete braid can now be marked and the working lines drawn. Do *not* transfer the pattern on to pricking card when the pin-hole markings are complete. Although it may appear as if they are all positioned correctly, it is often found that some of them need to be moved slightly to produce the required effect and, once a pin-hole is made in pricking card, it is there for life and cannot be altered. Remember that this type of lace is very flexible and does not depend entirely on rigid angles and lines on graph paper. The exact pin positions are not laid down by anyone but the designer. In fact, many sectional lace patterns are actually sold in the form of outline shapes in order that each lacemaker determines the pin positions for herself as the work progresses. If the design is intended to be worked a number of times or if the lace pillow is not rock hard, then it is advisable to put pricking card under the paper pattern, and a final, permanent pricking is made at the same time as the lace. If the pillow is really hard and the design is to be worked only once, a piece of ordinary stiff card is all that is required under the tracing.

By the way, do not forget to lay your tracing *upside down* on the card in order to produce a piece of lace which is the right way up when finished. It is also an excellent idea to put a piece of graph paper between the card and tracing paper. This not only helps to maintain the accuracy of the distances between the pin-holes and the width of braid, but also, if a filling stitch is to be worked, the grid for marking it is already in position.

Varying braid textures

When working the outline braid, variety can be achieved in several ways without adding any more passives. Straight edges can be worked for areas such as the legs which require a smooth outline or these parts can also be worked in ten-stick. Picots on the outside edge can depict an extra furry section or represent a mane. Sections can also be worked in half stitch or whole stitch and twist to alter the density of the braid where part of the animal is to the rear and in shadow. This is particularly useful if the thread is a light colour and the background is dark, and it helps to produce a three-dimensional effect.

Filling stitches

Having mastered the complexities of the outline braid, now let us discuss the filling stitches which can be used. If possible, these should reflect the texture of the animal or bird and the line of the threads should attempt to follow the lie of fur or feathers. It is best not to make these fillings too fancy, though, or they will draw the eye away from the main shape. The *Book of Bobbin Lace Stitches* by Bridget M. Cook and Geraldine Stott (*see* Further Reading list) is a boon for lace designers and is invaluable when choosing stitches to obtain the desired effect. Torchon Ground, Dieppe Ground are some of the most effective ones to use, although the various types of Spider fillings and Rose Grounds are also extremely successful. When deciding which stitch is the best, consideration must be given to the density of that stitch. When using a pale shade of thread, for example, the parts of the animal which are to the fore and not in shadow must have a greater density to give the impression of light. Those stitches to the rear should be more open because the background material should be dark and this helps to provide any shading needed. Conversely, a creature made in darker thread tones and mounted on a light background material will probably require a more open stitch to the front and a closer one to the rear. In this way, the background material

assists in producing any necessary shading by showing through the less dense stitches.

It is frequently possible to carry the threads of the filling stitches across from one area to another rather than to cut them off and start again in the next section. Be very careful, though, not to allow these threads to be seen on the right side of the work. Although the animal is solid, lace is not, and any part to the fore must not allow any rear working threads to show through. When using several different colours within the one animal, this is even more important. Just imagine a dark brown leg with pale green threads showing through in a haphazard fashion!

The White Horse

It is always preferable to draw an animal or bird in an action pose rather than a static one, in order to produce a piece of work with more interest and vitality. After all, animals are rarely completely still, except when asleep. The White Horse (pricking 26) was drawn from a school badge and enlarged in the same way as the camel. The thread used was BOUC 100 Fil de Lin with black DMC Brillante d'Alsace 30 for the nostrils and eye. It incorporates some of the ideas just mentioned and has a very lively appearance, not being as quiescent as the camel. The horse is depicted in the act of rearing, which gives life and movement to the design, and the outline braid width is variable. The technique of Schneeberg lace is used to give the tail realism by working a straight plaited edge on top. The width of the free-flowing hairs of the tail is controlled by the number of twists on the worker threads. A single filling stitch is introduced but is kept very simple. It is used solely to represent the body of the animal and to differentiate between the space outside the outline and the solid animal inside it.

Fig. 22. 'White Horse' – a design with 'movement' which was inspired by a blazer badge

Pricking 26. 'The White Horse'

Sleeping Mouse

A completely different approach is required for a composite picture such as the Sleeping Mouse design (pricking 27). The animal here is only one small, though integral, part of the overall picture. It requires a number of various coloured threads of the same thickness as DMC Brillante d'Alsace 30. The idea originated on a greetings card and the main shape was drawn free-hand (not traced). The coloured picture shows the original card and the finished lace together so that the changes which have been made can be clearly seen. When using an idea in this way, it is important to eliminate any superfluous sections of the original design so that only the essential framework is used. This prevents unnecessary embellishment which would be very confusing when working the lace. When making a decision about which parts of a picture are not required and are to be omitted, first of all decide what the most important features are and draw the outlines of these. This will produce the silhouette mentioned in the section on Line and Space. Now any ancillary parts (the structure lines) that are essential to

Fig. 23. *'Sleeping Mouse' – the greetings card which has the original design is shown here together with the finished lace*

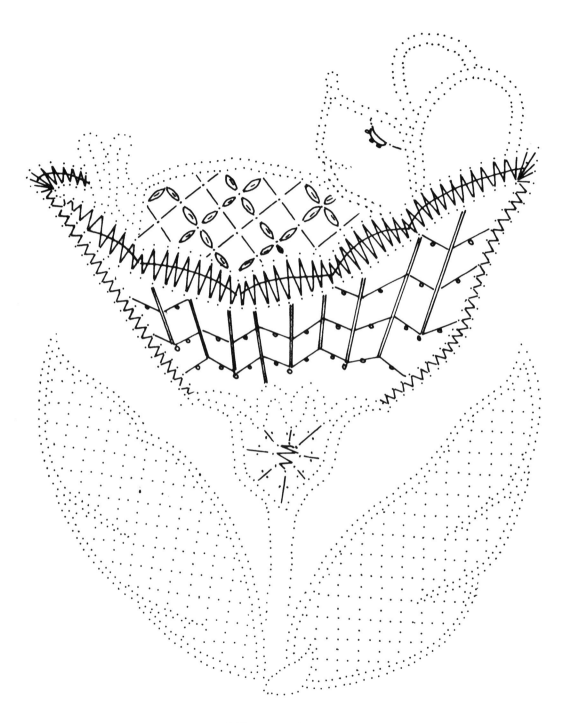

Pricking 27. *'Sleeping Mouse'*

the major features can be drawn. And lastly, the shading can be marked. By working thus, in descending order of importance, it soon becomes clear which parts can be omitted because they are superfluous and just unnecessary fripperies. In this way, a good shape for development emerges without any surplus embellishments.

The different elements of the design are worked in a variety of ways. The flower requires Schneeberg techniques and is worked in one piece, whilst the large leaves are constructed by working a braid outline and a filling stitch. The small leaf is worked in a single unit, and the feet, ears and face of the mouse are merely braid outlines with no fillings at all. The blanket and flower stem are both worked by making the centre filling at the same time as the outline braid. By combining various techniques in this way, more interest is given to the design and its various components are more distinct.

Facial expressions

At this point, it is worthwhile looking at the methods of obtaining facial expressions. Any faces that are required can be complicated in execution if great care is not taken. Unless the face is to be embroidered or painted on to the background material after the lace has been completed, it is better merely to indicate the features rather than to attempt any very great detail. If the design is of a head only and the features are essential to the overall picture, there is more room to manoeuvre the threads. The eyes are the most important component of a face as they control any required expression. Their shape, angle and position on the face can change the whole character and the intended emotions. Frequently, the eyes alone are the main feature by which a creature is identified. For example, the eyes of an owl dominate the face and are its main feature. Likewise, on a frog, the position and shape of its eyes, high up

and bulging on the top of its head, make its identity unique.

Working eyes in lace

There are a number of different ways of depicting eyes in a piece of lace. They depend upon the intended expression and whether the face is in profile or viewed from the front. Some of the methods that can be used are described below. Refer to diagram 18.

(i) A simple tally can be worked and the expression altered by the size and shape of it. A fat Maltese-type tally gives a very wide-awake look, whilst a crescent-shaped one with picots for eyelashes make the animal appear to be asleep. In this manner, the varying degree of width of tally changes the animal's mood. The angle at which it is positioned also changes its expression. By slanting it down towards the mouth it can appear more 'snooty' whilst the opposite effect can be made with a slant in the other direction.

(ii) If the head is being worked as a single piece of cloth stitch, the eye can be indicated by a hole or gap. Once again, it is essential that this space is in the correct position in relation to the rest of the head. When drawing the pattern for the eye, do not just indicate the position with a dot or scribble. Mark in the exact shape of the eye and then the final effect will be far more accurate and realistic because its correct shape is clearly visible whilst working the lace.

(iii) If the face is large in size, relative to the thickness of thread being used, it can be most effective to work the eye as a separate piece of ten-stick or narrow braid. This is worked in the exact shape required. Then any stitches or other fillings can be made round it afterwards, making sewings to attach the eye at appropriate places. A pupil can be added, if required, by working a

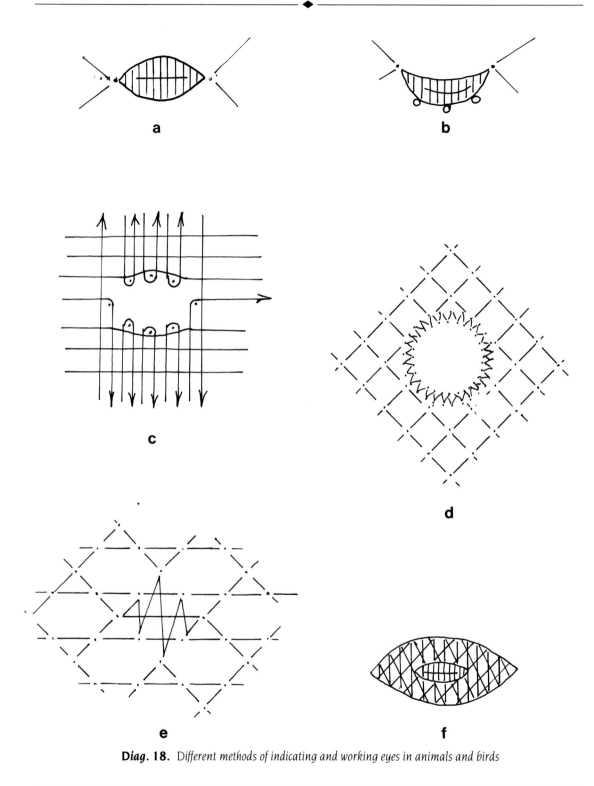

Diag. 18. *Different methods of indicating and working eyes in animals and birds*

tally vertically across the eye shape, to give more realism.

(iv) When working an open filling stitch within a braid outline for the head, the eye can either be indicated separately or formed using the same threads as the filling and at the same time. A section of the filling is worked in whole stitch to mark the places where the eye should be. Diagram 18*e* shows how this would be done if the filling were in Honeycomb Ground but it works just as well with other ground stitches.

(v) A realistic eye can be worked as a half stitch area with a raised tally to denote the pupil. Great care must be taken when doing this so that the tally is worked *under* the half stitch and not on top as is usually the case, because (remember) the underside is the right side.

(vi) If preferred, a bead can be used to indicate the eye instead of any of the above methods. It can either be worked with the thread or sewn in afterwards. For true realism, eyes which are intended for use by soft toy makers can be purchased from most craft and hobby shops and put in position.

(vii) When working the eyes for an owl, two completely separate sections must be made. The large area round the outside is really not the eye but a grouping of feathers and must be worked independently to the central pupil, although this inner part can sometimes be left blank and a piece of material or a bead can be used instead.

In general, front view eyes need more detail than profile eyes and frequently involve at least two different sections of working. Sometimes a more realistic eye can be made by using more than one colour of thread. The position of the pupil and its size within the shape of the eye is important and can change an emotion. Even putting a few eyelashes in the design can alter the whole expression of a face. Cartoon characters such as those found in newspapers and the Disney-type films can be studied to help an understanding of how eyes can be drawn. These are only some of the different ways of working eyes in lace animals and birds and there are, no doubt, many others.

Noses and mouths

Noses are usually worked in conjunction with mouths and form a snout for most animals, but the line and shape of these must be carefully made. An upward curve of the mouth will produce a happy expression whilst a downward one depicts sadness. If the mouth is drawn as a thin straight line, it may give an impression of severity. The working of the beaks of birds alters expression, too. The angle which the beak makes with the head on a profile, or the difference between an open beak and a closed one, can indicate different moods.

Any designer who intends to make patterns for a number of different animals and birds would do well to make a sampler of the different methods of obtaining the required effects and expressions for facial features. This can then be used as a reference in the future. These features can be the making or marring of a good piece of work as they are the focal points of any creature.

9 · Lace and embroidery

Designs for embroidery and lace have always developed along parallel lines. When researching into historical archives, the existence of so many pieces of work which demonstrate this prove that this evolution is no accident. In fact, there are recorded instances where a lace has been specifically designed to complement an embroidered garment. Santina Levey, in her book Lace, A History, tells us that in the Victoria and Albert Museum in London there are examples of Italian woven silk material and a Flemish bobbin lace, both of the 1660s, where the designs are very similar. Similarly, needle and bobbin laces from Flanders in the mid-seventeenth century show remarkable resemblances to one another. Not only were the aristocracy and churchmen wearing clothes that reflected this, but seventeenth-century examples of domestic bobbin laces made specifically to match domestic embroideries can be seen from countries as far apart as Portugal, Italy and England.

Some of the very earliest pattern books for embroidery were also intended for use as needle-made laces. The only designs for bobbin lace definitely known to have been included in these is in a book published in Venice in 1557. It can be seen that, making allowances for the dictates of the fashion world, the bucks and belles of the courts of Europe in past centuries wore very elaborately embroidered clothes embellished with lace collars, cuffs, jabots and frills, and the same shapes were reproduced in both fabrics in order to produce a continuity of design. It is very interesting for the lacemakers of the late twentieth century to experiment with this past work in order to produce some modern examples.

Jacobean designs

Ever since the seventeenth century, needleworkers have been fascinated by the magnificence of the designs and the glorious colour schemes produced by the Jacobean embroiderers. They were originally influenced by the Oriental techniques and patterns which were to be found in the printed fabrics brought to England at this time. This eastern influence, combined with the traditional Tudor decoration of delicate floral shapes, produced the distinctive designs and colours of Jacobean embroidery. Many of these shapes can be converted to make extremely attractive and delicate lace patterns. The fancy stitchery can also be followed to a large extent due to the wealth of coloured threads available to the modern lacemaker. In the original embroideries the predominant colour is green, which can be found in a large number of shades. The embroiderers also used many blues, browns and soft red tones. They did not necessarily use these colours in a naturalistic way, but rather than imitating nature worked them in many unusual combinations.

These designs were not restricted to embroideries and fabrics intended for wear. In Breamore House, a lovely Elizabethan manor house in Hampshire, a beautiful English pile carpet is displayed. This has the date 1614 woven into it. The design is a rich pattern of scrolling stems bearing a variety of flowers and fruit which are some of the shapes we normally associate with Jacobean designs.

Fantasy Bird
The idea for the Fantasy Bird (pricking 28) originated from a Jacobean wall-hanging. If a

Fig. 24. *'Fantasy Bird' – this has been designed from a small motif on a Jacobean wall hanging and is worked in tones of turquoise*

lace designer were to make a study of the weird and wonderful shapes and colour combinations to be found on these fabrics in our stately homes and museums, the time and effort expended would soon prove to be invaluable. In this particular case, different tones of turquoise have been combined with a metallic thread of the same colour, but an equally interesting experiment could be made with other colours which would produce completely different effects. The use of half stitch has prevented the area of the feathers becoming too solid and has also contributed to the curved lines of the arched neck. By adding metallic thread for the leg, beak and wing outlines, these parts are highlighted but not allowed to become dominant. The thread used is the equivalent of DMC Brillante d'Alsace 30.

When wishing to design a similar type of motif, usually very little adaptation need be made to the main original shape. Once the basic outline has been drawn from the embroidery, it must be ascertained which stitches were used and in which direction they were worked. This will give an insight into which lace stitches are required and in which direction they must travel in order to attain a similar effect. There are a number of lace stitches which bear a great resemblance to Jacobean embroidery fillings. As so much bobbin lace was developed during the same era as these embroideries, this is not really so surprising. The order in which the sections of the motif will be worked is still the same as when working an animal in lace – i.e. the parts to the foreground must be completed before those to the rear. Here, again, each section can be worked in one piece with no separate outline braid. Alternatively, a narrow edge shape can be worked by using ten-stick or plait which forms a smooth outline and is worked at the same time as the centre filling. Of course, the lace can be made without any separate colours, especially if the design is to be a part of a larger piece of work. In which case, it will probably not be possible to use a large number of different colours, and the required effect will have to be attempted solely with the thread in which the whole piece of lace is made.

Cross-stitch embroidery

Cross-stitch embroidery is one of the oldest methods of decorating fabric. From earliest times, this type of work has been done by needlewomen from peasants to royalty and a rich store of traditional designs has emerged. Originally, the patterns were very individual and each embroidress invented her own designs, but by the sixteenth century books of patterns were being printed.

Pricking 28. *'Fantasy Bird'*

Many of these patterns were very simple and worked in a single colour but cross-stitch embroideries used in court circles or by the Church became lavishly decorative works of art. The majority of the traditional peasant designs depicted the religious symbols and motifs of cross, stars and tree of life. Presumably, these were intended to fend off the demons and witches that bedevilled the folklore in ancient times.

Because cross-stitch embroidery designs have a very angular appearance, it could be presumed that they are of no practical use to a bobbin lacemaker who requires flowing curved lines. This is basically true, but it is very simple to adapt these shapes from one medium to the other. It is possible to purchase damask material with sections woven in it which are intended to be decorated with cross-stitch patterns. In this way, a lace can be designed perhaps as a border to complement such an embroidery. Because the designs are separated by a reasonably large area of material, the embroidery has less of an angular appearance and the two can combine to produce a pleasing harmony.

Alternatively, a cross-stitch design worked on a Binca or Aida material can be complemented by the use of a frame of Torchon lace. This type of lace can be used to great effect in conjunction with cross-stitch. The geometry of both is so compatible that the shapes within their design can be remarkably similar. When analysed, it can be seen that the cross on the material forms an angle of 45° with the warp and weft of the threads used to weave it. This is the same angle at which Torchon patterns are worked to the straight edge. Therefore, any shapes produced in the cross-stitch can, in theory, be iterated in Torchon patterns. Do not attempt to reproduce an entire design, though, but merely select one or two of the main elements for the lace pattern.

To explore this theory further, as an exercise take a piece of graph paper and plot out a small

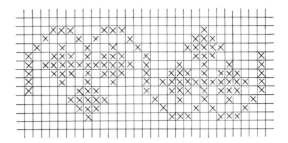

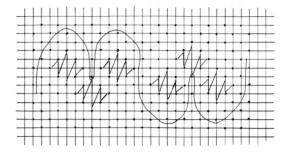

Diag. 19. *Comparison of shapes for cross-stitch embroidery and Torchon lace pattern*

cross-stitch motif. Now draw the same outline again, this time plotting it as a Torchon lace pricking. An example of the working of this is shown in diagram 19. A section of a border which can be found on a sample in the Bavarian National Museum in Munich, which depicts flowers and a continuous stem, has been plotted out and the same shape reproduced as a Torchon pattern. The flowers would be worked in whole stitch and the stem could be a gimp thread.

Heart design

An extension of this is depicted in figure 25. The theme of this piece of work is a heart. This particular shape is very adaptable in a number of different craft techniques. In this instance, two different cross-stitch designs have been used. The central one is a more elaborate version of the heart and serves to produce a focal point for the overall design, whilst the edging pattern is a simple repetitive one. The

Fig. 25. 'Little Hearts' – a mat with cross-stitch designs – three alternative edgings in bobbin lace are shown for comparison

Torchon lace edge repeats the hearts and the zigzag lines of the border embroidery. By using Dieppe ground, the emphasis is laid on the diagonal nature of the thread positions for both crafts.

You will see from the photograph that there are three different edge designs of lace shown for this mat. The outer two have been rejected as unsuitable in favour of the one that is actually attached, but they have been included as examples of incorrect design or execution. The colouring of all three pieces of lace is correct, but the outermost one uses a thicker thread so that there are less repeats of pattern, which does not produce a correct balance with the embroidery. Also, the cardinal sin of following one ground immediately with another has been effected at the outer edge. The central and inner pieces of lace show an identical pattern but can be used as comparisons between correct and incorrect stitches and threads. When examining them, it can be seen that the inner one is made using a thicker thread and the hearts are worked in cloth stitch rather than half stitch as in the middle one. This produces a far better balance in the design and

Fig. 26. *'Blue Bird' – note the slight differences between the cross-stitch original design and the finished bobbin lace version*

Pricking 29. *'Blue Bird with Olive Branch'*

makes the heart shapes themselves more prominent. Another small point to note, which helps to produce a better piece of lace, is the use of a 'nook' pin to take the gimp of the heart down into the cloth stitch at the indentation. On both outer pieces of lace there is an untidy hole between the gimp and heart centre at this point.

When producing work of this type, it is essential to use the same colours throughout. The base colour of the material centre must be exactly reproduced either as the main colour of the edge lace or as the gimp, and any colour introduced into the edge must be the same as the cross-stitch, or the reverse; i.e. the embroidery thread colour should be identical to the main lace thread. This means that if the material is cream rather than white, the lace thread should be also. If it were to be white, it could give the impression that the centre material is grubby or faded. When choosing which coloured threads to use, try to select a thread which has the same colour made in a variety of different thicknesses. For example, the DMC company produces threads of the same colour in Brillante d'Alsace, Fil à Dentelle, and Coton Perlé thicknesses. This means that the continuity of colour is kept. If the central cross-stitch is made in a variety of colours, it is better to keep the lace to the one colour which is the same as the material. Remember that the lace, in this instance, is acting as a frame or accessory to the embroidery and is not the main feature, so it should not bring attention to itself, but merely reflect the main feature.

Blue bird

Instead of drawing a design to complement an embroidery, the blue bird with an olive branch has been adapted directly from a cross-stitch pattern (see pricking 29). The original motif came from Switzerland and is one of the traditional designs of that country. Some of these patterns have been published by Batsford

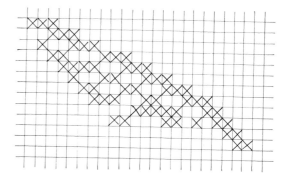

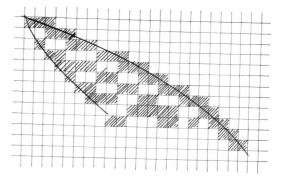

Diag. 20. *Drawing a lace design outline from a cross-stitch pattern*

in a book entitled *Cross Stitch Patterns* by Irmgard Gierl. Figure 26 shows the embroidered and bobbin lace versions side by side so that a true comparison of the shapes can be made. In these two pieces, the same thread (DMC Brillante d'Alsace 30) was used for the bird and branch in both, but the silver tails needed different threads. It is virtually impossible to produce a good cross-stitch tension using metallic threads which have been made specifically for lacemaking. These threads are much stiffer than those intended for use by embroiderers and cannot be pulled evenly through material. Conversely, metallic threads intended for embroidery do not always hold their shapes well when used in bobbin lace. For more information on metallized threads, refer to the section that deals with the use of them.

To produce a lace pricking from a cross-stitch pattern, the following method can be used.

It is best to draw the line through the centres of the squares as much as possible rather than at one edge or the other, so that a mean average line is produced. Any other method would produce a finished shape either too large, too small, or otherwise out of proportion. At this stage, only draw in the essential outline shape and then the structure lines, in a similar way to the Sleeping Mouse in the previous section.

The unnecessary parts of the design (such as the leg/foot and extra twiggy parts of the branch) which detract from the main shape have been ignored, but the shapes of the wing feathers have been maintained as this is part of the bird's structure. The flowing curves of the tail have become more fluid in the lace version, replacing the very angular appearance of the original embroidery.

When considering the filling stitches for this type of creature, care must be taken to put them at the correct angle and they should not all be worked in the same direction. If you study the bird, you can see that each wing is at a different angle to the horizontal and that the body is at yet another angle (see diagram 21a). It is most important to allow any filling stitches to follow these lines in order to obtain the correct 'line of flight'. When plotting these, each separate element must be drawn independently, with the central vertical axis of the stitches along this line. It is incorrect merely to place one single grid under the whole motif and to use this for the entire filling. In a similar way, a flower with petals radiating independently round a centre focal point must have the stitches flowing directly to the centre from the tip of each petal (see Diagram 21b). It is only in this way that a design will look more realistic.

Chrysanthemum

Here we have a small piece of embroidery in a large frame consisting of bobbin lace. The linen or cloth stitch of the lace is echoed in the satin stitch of the embroidered motif and both use

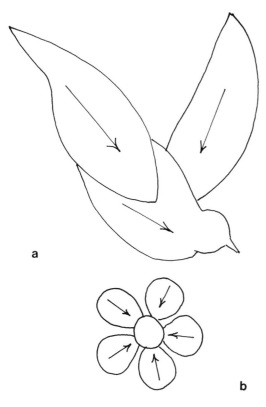

a

b

Diag. 21. *Positioning the axis for filling stitches*

Usually the original design is marked on small squares. This is very difficult to adapt so the design should be reproduced on paper with large squares. The best size of squares to use is 5mm. If the intention is to work the lace to a smaller size, it is quite simple to reproduce the finished pattern by reducing it on a photocopying machine. When drawing the cross-stitch design on to this larger squared paper, rather than putting a cross in each appropriate square, fill the whole space in. This gives a more realistic impression of where the solid parts of the design will be required. Once every square has been plotted, the shape will be far more distinct than if only a cross is marked.

Now place a piece of tracing paper over the drawing you have just completed and begin to smooth out the main outline (see diagram 20).

the same thread and have remarkably similar shapes. Usually, when working a pattern which combines these two techniques, the major feature of the design will be the embroidery, as it is in the 'Heart' mat, and the lace will be subordinate to it. In this case, though, we have the reverse, and the embroidery is used to supplement the main theme of the scrolls rather than used as the focal point itself.

The importance of tension and a sufficient number of passive threads is demonstrated very clearly in this design. Each of the petals is independent of the others and, therefore, relies upon its own inner thread tension to retain its shape when taken off the pillow. Referring to

pricking 30, the maximum number of passive pairs across each shape at any place is ten, when working with a thread of the thickness of DMC Brillante d'Alsace 30. The shapes of the scrolled petals are all slightly different but they create an overall circular outline. If they were to form a square shape, it would look incongruous, but they could be drawn to make an oval or pear shaped design with the central feature re-positioned accordingly. The size of the scrolls will also vary and a similar design could be made which would look most attractive. The

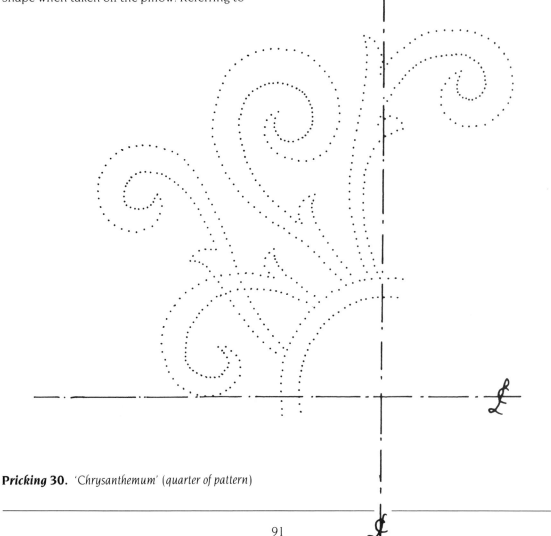

Pricking 30. *'Chrysanthemum' (quarter of pattern)*

most important thing is to put the focal point in the correct place, so that the straight lines, drawn across the diameters of the design from one edge to another, will all pass directly through it. Once this point is decided upon, the position of the petal shapes can be marked and the design completed. A comparison can be made with imaginary lines formed when working a piece of lace using Tenerife techniques. Whatever the final outer shape of the design, all the radiating threads will pass across one single point which is then used as the central commencement point for the weaving stitches.

Fig. 27. *'Chrysanthemum' – an experiment in tension and colour tones*

10 · The use of colour

It has been said in recent years that if a lace design is called 'modern' it must be worked in colour. This is a complete fallacy. There are fashions in the world of lacemaking just as in other spheres. I am quite sure that the lacemakers who lived in the second half of the seventeenth century would not agree that coloured lace is new to the twentieth century. There still exist some excellent pieces of lace which were made then and worked in beautifully coloured silk threads. Indeed, most of the very earliest bobbin laces were worked using linen and silk threads in the primary colours.

Lace designs and usage have always been, and still are, closely linked to the fashion industry. One year, perhaps, everyone is making lace flowers; the next year all the new lace produced has colour; and the following year bobbin lace is forsaken for the needle-made laces. It is very easy to let the tide of popular opinion carry you along, but much better to act with restraint and follow your own interests, and not be a sheep with the rest of the flock. Do not be persuaded that 'modern' equals 'colour'.

The worst reason for making a piece of lace in a number of coloured threads is that your friend is doing so or you want to 'keep up with the Joneses'. This can lead to a lacemaker choosing colours at random with no thought as to why or how she is doing this. There is only one good reason for using coloured or textured threads and that is to enhance a design in order to bring life to a piece of work that could appear flat or uninteresting otherwise. The belief that the whole pattern should be worked in colour to achieve this is also unfounded.

Frequently, a white handkerchief edging can be enhanced by adding a coloured worker pair

for the outside shell or fan, or even by the use of a coloured gimp thread. In order to follow the theme through the entire piece of work, these colours can then be reproduced as an embroidered motif on the centre material, or the material itself can be the secondary colour in the lace edging. Even the traditionally white Bucks Point patterns can have a coloured or metallic gimp thread to give them an extra sparkle, although this practice is heresy to the traditionalist. Why and how this has come about is, perhaps, a mystery that can only be answered by delving into the history of lace. After all, Pat Earnshaw tells us in her book *Lace and Fashion* of a lace pattern book published in Zurich in 1561 that 'specifies that many of the designs are to be constructed in gold and silver threads or in coloured silks'. So the dictates of fashion which required lace to be made in white, ecru or black have a lot to answer for.

Realistically, it would have been much simpler for the lacemaker of old to make coloured lace, as her standards of hygiene were so poor that her white lace was frequently very discoloured by the time it reached the lace merchants. This lace then needed treatment before its sale to bring it back to a pristine appearance. Once ecru coloured lace became fashionable, the lacemakers must have sighed with relief! The advent of black lace was probably greeted with mixed feelings. No need to worry so much about grime, but it must have been extremely difficult to see the work in progress by the light of a single candle.

It is worthwhile to make a study of colour before designing lace to be worked with a variety of tones. The understanding of how even a different shade of one colour can alter the intent of a piece of work should be attained before using coloured threads. By changing the colour of the material on which a piece of lace is displayed, a different emotion can also be represented. Most of us have knowledge of the colour wheel and have learnt of the three primary colours whilst still at school, but a simple reminder of this may be helpful.

The colour wheel

Refer to diagram 22 in conjunction with the table below for more clarity. The harmonious colours are those which lie adjacent to one

another on the colour wheel. When used together they blend well. For example, a design which has tones of blue through green to yellow will be attractive in appearance. Contrasting or complementary colours lie opposite one another on the wheel. They can be used side by side to great effect in a design. Examples of contrasting colours are red and green, or orange and blue. Discordant colours are brought together by upsetting the natural order. For instance, we know that red and orange are harmonious, as are red and purple, and that red is darker than orange. If white is added to red to make pink, then pink will be discordant with orange and is said to clash with it. Normally these two colours would not show up to advantage if put next to one another in a piece of work, and it is preferable to avoid this state of affairs if possible, unless the intention is to produce a conflicting colour effect.

Another useful feature of colours is their ability to produce an optical illusion of depth in a flat piece of work. If a section of a design needs to appear to recede into the background, a darker colour should be used. The use of a lighter colour brings that part of the pattern forwards. A flat design can be made to appear solid by using darker tones and paler tints and basing the whole on one colour only. When a section of the work needs to be highlighted, a brighter colour can be used and the rest toned down by adding a greyer thread. It is useful to remember that dark colours make objects

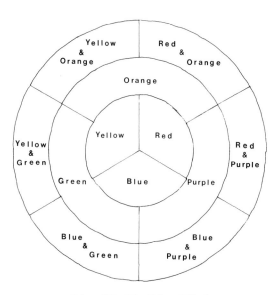

Diag. 22. *The Colour Wheel*

Primary colours	Secondary colours	Sub-secondary
blue		
	blue + yellow = green	blue + green
yellow		yellow + green
	yellow + red = orange	yellow + orange
red		red + orange
	red + blue = purple	red + purple
blue (again)		blue + purple

appear smaller than they are and light colours make them seem larger.

Background colours

The colour of any backcloth or base on which the lace is to be displayed is very important, too. If the wrong colour is used, it can completely destroy the illusion that is intended to be presented. For example, if a picture of some violets were to be worked with pale mauve flowers and green leaves, what would be the best background colour for it? This all depends upon the final impression required. By using a mauve or purple colour which tones with the flowers, the effect is warm and friendly; but if a pale green is chosen, the impression of a cool leafy glade is given.

The warm colours are those which predominate in red, orange and yellow whilst the cold colours are the blue and green tones. Gold thread can be added to give a little sunlight to a picture whilst silver will produce a frosty impression. Experimenting with a box of water colour paints can be a very rewarding experience for the lace designer. If one particular simple shape is chosen and photocopied a number of times, these copies can then be coloured in a variety of ways. In this manner, a portfolio of colour effects can be made which would help with colour choice at a later date.

Interchange of Colours

When designing a piece which will be worked in coloured threads, it can be helpful to consider all the various combinations of colour tones before actually working it, and in this way a more positive approach to the use of colour can be made.

By referring back to the 'Chrysanthemum' design in the previous section, the use of colour in this piece can be seen to be vital to its whole

appearance. By choosing the warm autumnal shades of yellow, orange and brown, the design takes on the appearance of a chrysanthemum. Not only do the shapes reflect those of that particular flower, but the colours used are also associated with the time of year when they bloom. These shapes could also be used in a representation of Spring, by choosing various tones of pink instead of orange, and the shapes can then be associated with the opening buds and unfurling petals at that time of year. Winter could also be represented by the same design if it were to be made in white and silver threads, which would give it the look of freshly fallen snow amongst the frosty fronds of fern on a forest floor. Alternatively, if shades of blue, green and turquoise were to be used, the coolness of a cascade of water with the frothing foam at its base can be imagined. So it is that colour can completely alter the whole mood of a design.

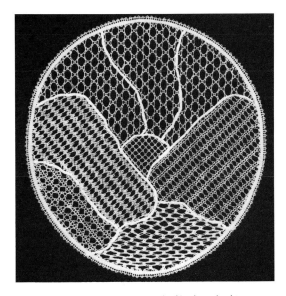

Fig. 28. *'Mountain Dawn' – the black and white version of the design*

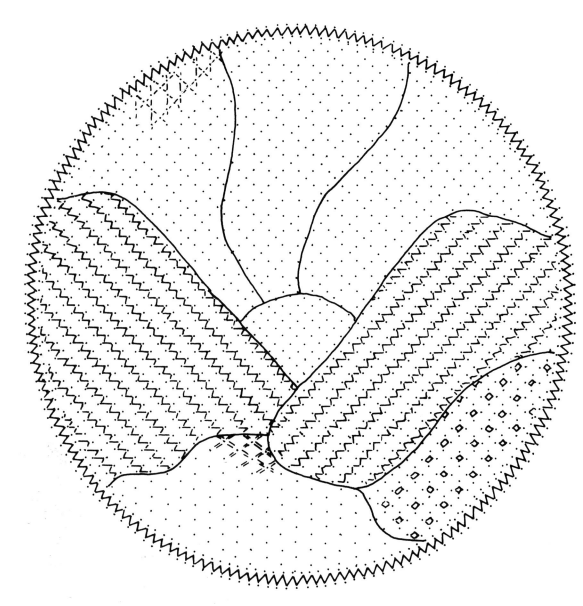

Pricking 31. *'Mountain Dawn'*

Mountain dawn

To illustrate the difference between a design which uses white threads only and one which contains a number of coloured threads within it, pricking 31 has been made. The actual pin-holes and stitches used are identical in each case, but the first version has been worked in white whilst the second has each section of the scene worked in a different realistic colour, as seen on the colour page. It is entirely up to the individual lacemaker which version she prefers, but most people agree that the colour has highlighted the picture so that it is immediately evident what the subject is without the need for

I. Dressing-table set and fan in Schneeberg lace: note the Bruges flower work mat, flower arrangements and wallpaper with similar shapes in their designs

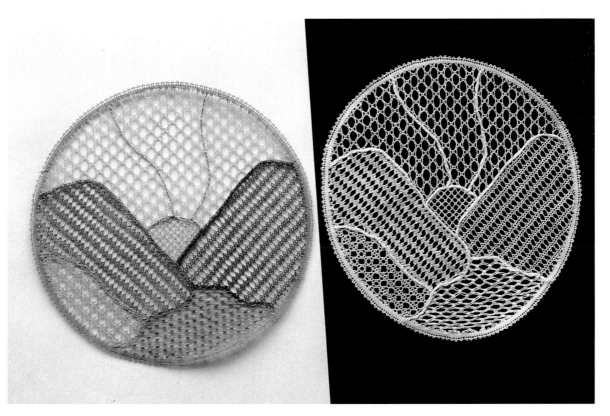

II. 'Mountain Dawn': the comparison of a white piece of lace and one made with identical stitches and pin-holes but using coloured threads

III. *Composition: the 'Thistle', a single garter and a set of coasters representing the four seasons*

IV. Candles: on this Christmas
card motif, the worker pair
for the edge braids is cotton,
whilst the rest of the threads
are metallized

V. 'Ring of Eternity': an
emerald-green braid lace
mounted on a cushion; the
design was derived from the
illuminated script in the
Book of Kells

VI. 'Blue Bird': a traditional
Swiss cross-stitch design
translated into bobbin lace

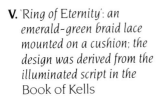

VII. *'Spider's Web': a picture incorporating various coloured and textured threads*

VIII. Flower Arrangement: *see the section on flowers to make a similar arrangement*

IX. 'Beautiful Beastie':
this originated as a
traditional cross-
stitch design. Note
the metallic eye
and tail

X. Welsh Dragon: note
the repetition of the
same filling stitches
in the dragon and
Torchon edging

XI. *Father Christmas: this charming animal was developed from a novelty greetings card. Note the dotted backing material to give the effect of falling snow*

XII. *Chrysanthemum: the yellow, orange and brown tones reflect the autumnal season*

XIII. *Sleeping Mouse: this shows how colour can animate a design*

a certain amount of imagination, which could be required when viewing the all-white version shown in Figure 28.

Choosing the correct mount/ frame for coloured lace

When contemplating the use of any frame or mount that will be used with a piece of lace, the colour of the mount and any design that may be on it is very important. It must be considered before any pattern is attempted. The lace must complement and reiterate any shapes and colours on the frame so that all is integrated. For instance, if a fan is to be made and the sticks are an ivory colour, the lace must be worked in a similar tone, and not in white which would clash and give the appearance that, perhaps, the sticks had become dirty. In the same way a set of white sticks should not be

mounted with cream lace. When deciding which thread would be the correct one to use, it is best to choose the thread in true daylight and not in artificial light. So-called daylight fluorescent tubes can give a false impression of colour tone and even ordinary electric light bulbs do not give a true picture. This can make all the difference as to whether to use a cotton or linen thread. Generally speaking, linen thread is whiter than cotton thread (although there are always a few exceptions) and quite often a half-bleach linen thread can be almost the same tone as a so-called white cotton one. The number of different whites in threads made by the various manufacturers is significant and great care must be taken when choosing the one that will be used to give the best final effect. It would be a great pity if, after all the hours of work that will be put into a piece of lace, it looks grubby and discoloured against its frame.

Fig. 29. *Brown and Gold Fan – this shows how the design and texture of the fan sticks are complemented in the lace*

Brown and gold fan

Referring to pricking 32 and figure 29, this fan pattern was made to match the sticks, which are brown with a gold design. This gold decoration meant that either the lace had to be made all in brown or, in order to make the lace more striking, the same shapes must be repeated within the design of the lace and outlined in gold to match the sticks. The final pattern has become a true 'Upminster' lace.

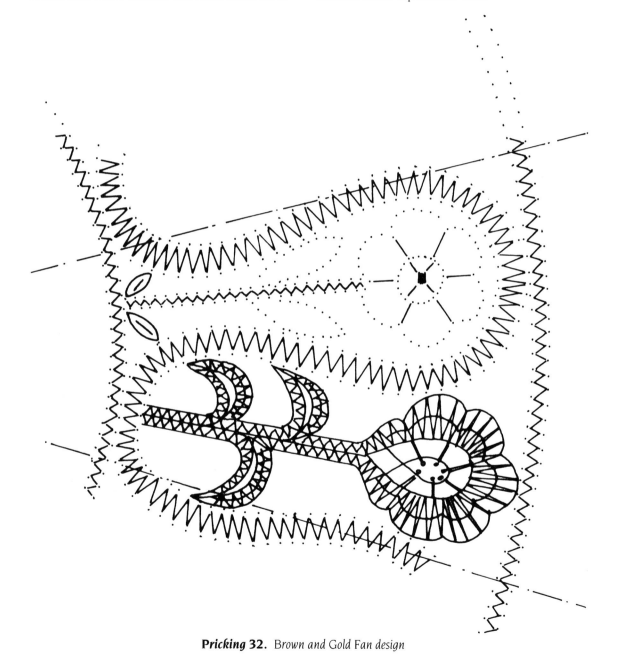

Pricking 32. Brown and Gold Fan design

Designing lace fans can be a very tricky business and the number of sticks has to be considered. An excellent booklet is available which gives some very helpful information and advice on this. It is written by Christine Springett and is entitled *Designing and Mounting Lace Fans*. It can be purchased direct from the British College of Lace (see address at the end of this book). Anyway, once the position of the sticks has been decided, the design can be sketched out using polar graph paper. It is best to draw the whole shape and not just to concentrate on one section, hoping that an exact number of repeats will fit.

The problem of the ever-widening radial lines has been overcome in this particular instance by the use of a meandering trail worked in Fil à Dentelle which is used as a bold framework for the design. It is strengthened by the use of the gold thread worked in chain stitch through the centre. The spaces enclosed by this trail have been filled with alternating Bruges and Schneeberg flowers and leaves. The thread for these is DMC Brillante d'Alsace 30 with Guttermann gold. This is finer than that used for the framework and trail in order to make the actual pattern more delicate, and to give more detail.

Finally, the ground has been worked in Tulle du Puy to obtain a mesh background which holds the various elements together. If required, this could be a single piece of machine-made net on to which the main design would be sewn. A large number of fiddly sewings are involved in working patterns in this way because the threads of the mesh filling cannot pass across

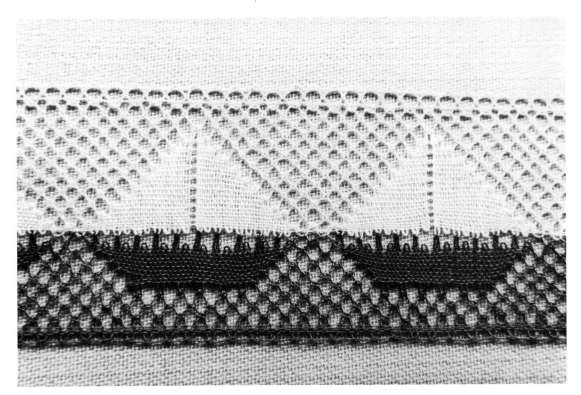

Fig. 30. *'Little Boats' – this piece demonstrates the use of four separate colours in one continuous length of Torchon lace*

the flowers and leaves. But the finished product is very delicate and the main shape of the gold pattern on the fan sticks has been echoed in the lace. When working two different thicknesses of thread together in one design in this way, the grid for the finer thread is smaller, and thus when the sewings are made into its thicker main outline, the correct positions are not always at the pins but can be made between them.

Little boats

A further exploration into the use of colour can now be made. Up to now the lace edgings that have been discussed have consisted of one main thread with a single colour introduced as a highlight. These are instances where a second subsidiary colour can be added to a monochrome piece of lace. This can be used as a worker pair to colour a trail, edging fan or shell; or as a gimp thread. Now we can consider using a number of different colours all together so that each element which is not relevant to any other part is shown in its own particular colour.

The little sailing boats edging (pricking 33) depicts and demonstrates this very clearly.

Within this design four colours are used, and the pattern is divided into clear-cut sections by them. The sky is blue; the sails white; the boat brown and the sea a greeny-blue colour. When working a braid lace, the threads which dominate and give it its colour are the passives, but in continuous laces which have only blocks of cloth stitch in their design, the worker threads can take over this role. So if the worker pair is wound with a different coloured thread from the passives, it submerges their colour and gives its own colour to that section of the work. Hence, the blue sky threads become submissive within the sails by the white worker pair. Similarly, the brown worker pair of the boat's hull overpowers the green passives threads from the water. Great care must be taken, though, at the place where these two worker pairs merely travel across from their own particular important sections. The stitches used for this may have to be adapted to prevent them travelling to the wrong place, in order to ensure that they are ready to take over again at the beginning of the next boat. In this way, the final appearance of the lace is evenly balanced with four colours.

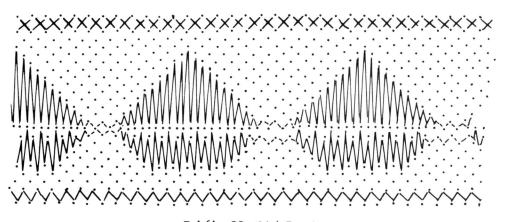

Pricking 33. *'Little Boats'*

11 · Texture and textured threads

When an object is touched, it can frequently be identified by its feel alone, and some of the distinctions between textures can be listed as follows: hard or soft; rough or smooth; thick or thin; cold or warm; shiny or matt, and solid or hollow. These can form a basis to work upon. Many threads can be listed under one or other of these headings, or even several of them, and it can be a rewarding experience to produce a piece of lace that not only resembles an object in looks, but also feels similar to it. A simple example of this is a three-dimensional rose worked in a coloured silk thread. If the petals are worked in cloth stitch and assembled at varying angles, they take on the look and the velvety-soft feel of a real rose. All you need is a sachet of dried rose petals nearby to produce a perfume, and it could almost be the 'real thing'.

Although they are given separate sections, colour and texture are inextricably entwined. Every single design relies on texture to a certain extent: whether the threads are shiny or matt, for example, or in the density of the stitches used. Therefore, it is incorrect to assume that texture is a topic set apart. There are a number of threads available nowadays which have a variety of depth and width, and these will produce a wealth of different effects which can be combined with the more traditional threads to give realistic textures to the lace.

It is essential to give careful consideration to the texture of a piece of lace and a design must always have varying degrees of texture built into it. This is even more important when using only one colour and a single thread type. If only one type of stitch is used throughout a piece of lace, the product is flat and uninteresting. The main features of the design should immediately be discernible and the background should be just that; no more. We all know that cloth stitch produces a good solid piece of lace whereas half stitch is more net-like and delicate. By using this knowledge and by working the first half of an edge fan in whole stitch and changing to half stitch for the second half, that section of the lace has been given more interest and depth.

So, when designing a piece of lace, the main features can be made more prominent by the use of cloth stitch and (perhaps) a thick gimp thread as an outline. Any part of the lace which adjoins the main pattern must be worked using an open-work stitch to allow it to recede and to separate the various elements within it. There is a large variety of stitches which can be selected for these subordinate sections, so that there should be no need for them to be uninteresting. In this way, although the main outline design is a solid cloth stitch, the background texture can be made more varied.

It is also vitally important not to allow one background stitch to follow another immediately without a section of the main design to separate them. There is little point in following an area of Rose Ground, for example, with Tulle du Puy; or Honeycomb Stitch with Spiders, unless it is to illustrate a very special point. None of the stitches would be shown up to the best advantage and the finished lace would just look messy. Always fill the spaces between each of the dominant elements with a single background stitch to give some texture to that part. Also, do not have too many different background stitches within the work. A piece of lace with a plethora of filling stitches has a very confusing appearance, but if they are well-chosen and correctly used, the work is enhanced by the texture produced.

Having discussed the ability to give lace a different texture by working chain stitch or stem stitch in a braid; or by using thick metallized threads combined with normal lace thread; or by changing the stitches themselves, now we can consider the use of those yarns which have their own built-in texture. Some of these work extremely well in conjunction with our more traditional threads, whilst others are best left strictly alone.

New textured threads

The late twentieth century is an exciting time for the lacemaker/designer. Lace has always depended upon the use of a variety of stitches to produce a mixture of textures, but today there are also numerous textured threads available as well. These combine with the traditional fibres and methods of producing a piece of lace with very interesting results. The opportunity for experimenting with threads of unusual texture and combining these with a myriad of colours is immense and when used in a variety of ways some exciting laces should emerge. We must be careful, though, that our enthusiasm does not exceed the bounds of credibility and forget the intrinsic nature of lace. A heavy, solid piece of fabric, however it is produced, and whatever interesting material is used in its making, can *never* be called 'lace'.

Thread manufacturers seem almost to vie with one another to produce the different textures and colour combinations within their wares. Unfortunately, some of the more unusual of these are only 'limited editions' and production ceases just when we have discovered their merits. This is especially true of

some of the more unusual yarns produced by wool manufacturers. Whenever there is a fashion for a particular type, they promote it with a very high profile, and then, some six months or a year later, it disappears from the shop shelves to fade into obscurity.

As already mentioned, when choosing any thread for a particular design, the type of thread is determined by the finish required and the background material or mount to be used. In order to assist in the choosing of the correct thread, it is useful to tabulate the various effects required and the methods of obtaining them and to keep a permanent record of these on file.

Types of thread

There are so many types of thread on the market today that it would be impossible to name every one. However, the following list can be used as a starting point for a designer. She can then make her own tabulation of the textures produced by traditional threads and some of the various texture combinations that can be effected by using these and the new threads available. We must start with the traditional natural fibres that have been used over the past centuries. These threads still make the very highest quality of lace which has durability and the ability to hold its shape. These qualities cannot always be found in man-made fibres as many lacemakers have discovered to their cost. The advantage that we have over our predecessors is in the variety of colour and thickness in the traditional threads now available to us. Many of us, though, have deep regrets that our present-day manufacturers cannot provide us with threads as fine as those once used.

(a) *Silk* – This is a shiny, soft thread. Light reflects on it to form shadows and produces a variety of colour depths at different angles.

◆

Beware of using bobbins with rough patches or working with it after doing the gardening or housework as silk thread snags very easily.

(b) *Metal* – These threads are rough and glittery. Their addition to a piece of work produces a sparkle, especially when they are the same colour as the main thread used. They are dealt with at length in the section on metallized threads.

(c) *Cotton* – This is a smooth, even-textured thread, produced from the fluffy seed heads of the cotton plant. Some of the 'gassed' cotton threads give a shiny effect but they usually produce less shine than a silk thread. The finished work may, on occasion, shrink from the original pattern size but it is a rewarding thread to use.

(d) *Linen* – Linen thread is made from the central fibres in the stem of the flax plant. This usually means that where a join has to be effected between two lengths of fibre in the manufacturing process, this part is slightly thicker than the rest of the thread. Some thread manufacturers are now trying to eliminate this visible join but I, personally, prefer the look of lace made with linen thread traditionally produced. This slight thickness can be an extra identifying feature when discovering with which type of thread a piece of lace has been made.

(e) *Wool* – This produces a soft, fluffy fabric which is warm yet light-weight to wear. The man-made wool-type lookalikes are especially good to use. They are dealt with at more length in the next section.

These five thread types are the more usual traditional ones that have been used for many years. Much is known of their behaviour in usage and the final effects that can be achieved with them, so let us now consider some of the

more unusual threads and their possible use by twentieth century designers. There are so many of these that they could not all be included here. Instead, I have attempted to choose a representative cross-section of them.

Effects obtained by using textured threads

Figure 31 shows the effects produced on a simple Torchon design using three different types of thread. Each has its advantages and disadvantages and has no second thread used in its construction.

(a) The design at the top is worked in a Boucle type of cotton/wool mixture. Of the two diamond shapes in the centre, one has been worked in cloth stitch and the other in half-stitch, but there is very little apparent difference

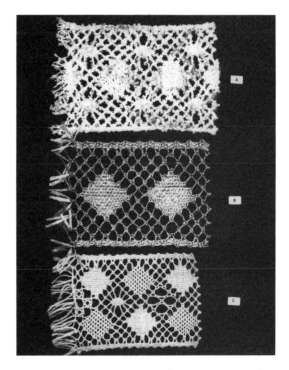

Fig. 31. *Torchon lace samples using a variety of textured threads:* (a) *Bouclé wool,* (b) *Raffia,* (c) *wool/linen mixture thread*

between them. It is a nice firm fabric but the outline of the features is not very distinct.

(b) The centre sample is worked in raffia. This is a very unusual material for a bobbin lace worker to use. The finished product is as stiff as a board and would make excellent table mats, etc., as the outline is clear and there is no shrinkage, but (and there is a big 'but'), I have not yet discovered a method of persuading the strips of raffia to retain the slip knot on the bobbins. This is a distinct disadvantage and much time is wasted rewinding running threads! If only this problem could be solved..........

(c) This thread is made of 50 per cent wool and 50 per cent linen. It is intended to be used as a knitting yarn but it works very well in bobbin lace, too. It has a considerably rough appearance and the 'woody' bits can be seen in the spaces between the stitches. This is an ideal thread to use to depict the rough cement walls of a house, for example, and it holds its shape well.

Figure 32 shows four of the effects of various textured threads used in conjunction with a more traditional one. Whenever a new design is to be made, a sample piece of the threads which are to be considered should be made working a piece in cloth stitch. In this way, a file of samples can be collated and constantly added to with reference made to the distances between the pin-holes, etc.

(a) This top piece uses BOUC Fil de Lin 50 as its main thread. A single bobbin wound with a Chenille type thread is used instead of a worker pair for the cloth stitch central zigzag section. This thread is a most interesting one to use and the finished part of the lace worked in it is soft and velvety to the touch and is also slightly raised. It would make an excellent gimp thread, too.

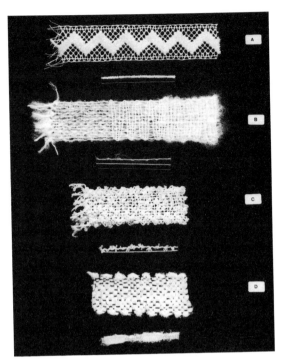

Fig. 32. *More examples of the use of textured threads*

(b) This sample is a different kettle of fish. The passive threads consist of a mohair wool yarn. This is very fluffy and moults continually. Three different types of worker thread have been used. At the right hand side the worker is the same mohair wool thread; the centre is made using a Coton Perlé worker pair; whilst at the left hand side a silver metallic thread has been used. In this way, the amount of fluffiness has been controlled and reduced as required.

(c) Here we have the Boucle yarn which was used alone in Figure 31. This time the amount of roughness which the loops produce has been tempered by the use of a Coton Perlé worker pair. Both this and the previous sample show how the texture can be regulated.

(d) The bottom sample is in complete contrast to the others. The worker threads are a yarn called 'Rags to Riches' and the passive pairs are wound in a black 60 crochet cotton. This has the effect of producing a brick-wall type of structure which has shiny and matt sections where the yarn changes. This type of thread is not recommended for use by itself. It is best used like the Chenille just to highlight a particular section of a design.

It can be seen from the above examples that the variety of textures obtainable using modern threads and yarns is very extensive. These are just the tip of the iceberg and when these, and other textured threads, are worked in conjunction with the multitude of available colours, some extremely interesting results can be produced.

Spider's web picture

In the eyes of a naturalist or a gardener, a spider's web will always seem equivalent to lace. No one can remain unaffected by the sight of early morning sunlight shining on a bedewed web. This picture attempts to capture this magic and to emphasize the menacing threat of the spider to the delicate and innocent butterfly. By combining threads with different textures and thicknesses a scene can be depicted with more realism and depth than if the entire design is worked in the same monotone thread throughout.

One should endeavour to be as realistic as possible. In this case it was necessary to discover the construction methods by which the spider makes its web to obtain maximum realism. Library books revealed that there are always an equal number of radial threads which the spider spins first. The circular thread is then commenced at the centre and is wound in ever-increasing circles round and round evenly until

Fig. 33. *'Spiders Web' – a picture consisting of various colours and textures*

the entire area is filled. Truly a magnificent achievement.

So, here in Figure 33, we have a picture of contrasts. The silky shine of the delicate web, for example, is the exact opposite in texture of the rough branches of the tree. The black predator at the base awaits the butterfly about to make a disastrous landing. Or is it? When designing this type of picture, try to give it a story, and not just make it a statement of fact. Here the spider has spent many patient hours making his trap and now awaits his reward, but the buttterfly has not yet landed, so the final outcome will never be known!

12 · Working with wool

The textures discussed in the previous section included some created by woollen threads, but we did not broach the many problems that can be encountered. At the risk of appearing repetitive, this section deals with them more specifically.

During the nineteenth century, a Torchon-type of lace using woollen thread was made commercially both in France and England. The title given to this family of lace in this country was 'Yak', but it was known as 'Lama' or 'Poil de Chevre' (goat) in France. This name was something of a misnomer as the English version was made of Yorkshire wool; nor was the French variety made from yak or goat's wool. It was thought to have originated in the Le Puy region of France but other areas quickly adopted this new lace form and it was extensively used for trimmings on furnishings and heavy-weight costume items from the 1850s onwards.

At the Great Exhibition in London in 1851, a section was devoted to so-called 'novelty' laces which included mohair and yak lace, both of the hand-made and machine-made varieties. Whereas some of the other 'novelty' laces died a natural death, the woollen ones became an established part of the lace trade for some years. Although these were usually made in black or dark brown wool, some was made in white and quite a lot was manufactured in other colours. The patterns were very simple, geometric ones and showed the influence of a Maltese, Cluny and Torchon ancestry. One of the failings of the original hand-made version was that it was very easily copied by the machine lace manufacturers and soon Yak, Lama and Mohair laces were being made in Nottingham, Cambrai and Calais. In this way,

the development of such a fast-growing method of making a coarse lace, which was intended to assist the hand-made industry, soon became a hindrance instead of the help originally intended.

The lacemakers did not really enjoy making lace with this woollen thread for several reasons. In the first instance, the scales on the fibres stuck together and it was very difficult to get an even tension in the work. Also, when the pins were removed and the lace lifted from the pillow, the elasticity in the wool made it shrink to some two-thirds of its original size. The weight of the wool, too, was such that it made the bobbins very heavy to use. It did not find favour with the purchaser/wearer either because it made a very itchy fabric when worn next to the skin and shrank badly when washed. Therefore, fashion designers had to give in to popular demand and woollen lace disappeared from the forefront of fashion.

We are more fortunate with our woollen threads in the late twentieth century. The invention of processes that prevent much of this shrinkage during laundering, and the discovery of methods to counteract the itchiness of natural wool, have improved the product considerably. Lambswool and Shetland wool both still need extra careful treatment in the cleaning process, but there are a number of man-made wool-type fibres and mixtures with natural wool which make very hard-wearing lace, and they retain their shape well.

Working with wool can still prove something of a difficulty in a number of ways, but these can usually be overcome and this medium can be a boon to those lacemakers who cannot use fine thread with petite patterns for various reasons, and yet still wish to enjoy the rhythm of

Fig. 34. A group of items made from woollen threads including the 'Ring of Eternity' cushion design

movement and satisfaction of achievement that making bobbin lace can provide.

Suitable wool types

There are, of course, some types of wool that are not really suitable for working in bobbin lace. Bouclé wool can be effective if worked in conjunction with a second smooth thread, but when worked alone, it has a habit of sticking to itself and the threads need to be pulled very carefully to give a good tension. On the other hand, a wool thread with this texture can be used to great effect if the passive threads only are in Bouclé and the worker threads are of a cotton or linen thread in the same colour or in complementing tones. The texture of tree trunks worked in this way is particularly effective providing the worker pair is wound with a thinner thread than the Bouclé passives. The bodies of spiders and other furry creatures can also be formed using these threads.

Mohair wool is one of the most difficult of all to work and I do *not* recommend it highly. Not only does it produce a messy, fuzzy fabric but it provides considerable problems on the bobbins themselves. Trying to maintain an effective slip knot can be a very frustrating experience and the finished lace does not seem to be worth all the trouble it has caused in the making. Once again, though, as with Bouclé wool, there is always the exception that proves the rule and there could be a limited use for it in conjunction with other threads.

Most ordinary wool makes a good, firmly textured lace. Normally, it is not a good idea to use threads that are not natural fibres when lacemaking unless they are used in conjunction with cotton or linen threads, but the acrylic yarn intended for use on knitting machines is an exception to this rule. It makes a very good bobbin lace and the finished work is extremely light, though warm to wear, if worked as a scarf, stole or even a jumper. In figure 34 we can see a group of articles which were made using woollen thread. The swan design on the cushion is most effective and is worked in this acrylic yarn. Many simple designs can be scaled up and used in this way. The two scarves are both worked in wool, one in double knitting and the other in a very fine 2-ply, whilst the large stole at the back is also made in yarn intended for use with knitting machines. The other cushion is the 'Ring of Eternity' design described in the section on braid laces.

Designing patterns to be worked in wool

When designing a pattern to be worked in wool, needless to say a very fine graph paper is not suitable. Grid lines of $^1/_8$ inch or more apart are required, although of course, the exact scale is determined by the thickness of thread to be used. This must always be decided upon by working the usual test piece because double knitting thickness yarns, in particular, can require a very large grid.

Care must also be taken to ensure that the stitches which are to be used are suitable for working in wool. As can be seen in figure 34, tallies look lovely as the leaves of the willow tree on the swan motif cushion. The fibres of the wool adhere to one another and it makes a good firm shape with an even outline. Unfortunately, wool is a very elastic medium in which to work and a good tension must be consistently kept on the threads whilst working them. It is worthwhile taking extra care with the tension to produce even ground stitchery and cloth stitch areas as any slight defect is considerably magnified when working the lace to such a large scale. The pulling to maintain the tension affects the work which has been completed some distance back so the pins must be left in for a greater length of work than when using finer threads. Also, the usual brass or stainless steel pins used by lacemakers are not manufactured with thick enough diameters. The wool makes them bend very easily so large, strong Berry pins are required instead to ensure that the work in held in the required shape.

Then there is also the problem of pillow size. It is very rare for a piece of lace being worked in wool to be small enough to use one of the 18 inch diameter flat pillows normally used, so a pillow of some 24 inch upwards is necessary for a round or square piece of work. Most of the Continental-type roller pillows are not wide enough, nor do they have a large enough diameter of roller to make a long continuous lace in a woollen thread, unless the pattern is to be worked in a number of very narrow strips which are intended to be sewn together afterwards. With roller pillows too, there is the problem that only a short length of pins can be left in the work and the finished part may be distorted whilst keeping the required tension on the threads. Therefore, a block pillow, with the blocks wide enough to take the design in one piece, is a good investment; or, alternatively, a large bolster pillow can be used to prevent more time being spent in moving the pattern up than in making the lace.

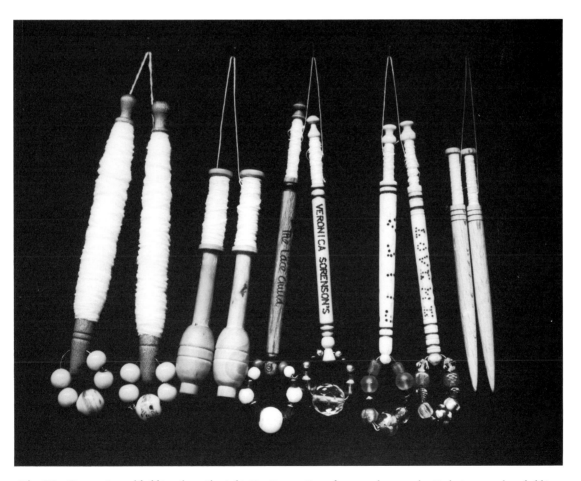

Fig. 35. *Comparison of bobbins: from the right, Honiton, antique bone, modern wooden Beds-type, modern bobbins from Belgium, large-size Beds-type wound with wool*

Bobbins, too, can prove to be a problem when using wool. Figure 35 shows a comparison between various types of bobbins fully wound with thread. They range from a pair of bobbins used for making Honiton lace; through antique bone bobbins, modern Bedfordshire-type bobbins and bobbins from Belgium; to a larger Bedfordshire-type wound fully with wool. It can be seen that those wound with the woollen thread become almost submerged as if they are balls of thread themselves. If only the neck of the bobbin is used, less thread is wound on to them and there will be many joins in the finished lace. These are not only ugly to look at but weaken the finished fabric. Care must be taken, though, especially if working with white or pale coloured wool, that the threads are not handled too much. Do not keep pulling the threads tight after each block of work but only handle the bobbins as each stitch is made. The threads will then quite easily position themselves correctly at this juncture.

Length of thread required

When wool has been used to make a bobbin lace scarf or stole, the finished article provides a lot of warmth without weight. The amount of air encompassed by the yarn increases the warmth, and the fact that surprisingly little length of yarn is needed prevents the weight from becoming too much. This is a fact with all bobbin lace. It uses far less thread per square metre than any of the single thread laces. Although it may seem that a lot of thread is required whilst winding the many bobbins that are involved, when the final length is measured, far less has actually been used. When this phenomenon is analysed, it comes down to the basic methods of construction. Crochet, for example, consists of a single thread which is looped round and over itself a number of times to make a single stitch. Knitted lace is also a looped fabric which uses more thread length

per square metre than bobbin lace. Needlepoint, Tenerife and Tatting techniques also involve a single thread being manipulated over and around itself and use a considerable length to make relatively small pieces of lace. Bobbin lace, however, is produced by a flat woven procedure and no area of it is more than a single thread in depth except where two threads pass directly over one another. Thus the finished piece of work is much lighter to wear and holds its shape when laundered.

'Spiders and diamonds' scarf

The scarf (pricking 34) worked in Patons 'Fairytale' double knitting wool was made on the bias and much of the width was lost in shrinkage as it was taken off the pillow. After it had been pinned out and pressed with a warm iron into the correct size, it regained its original measurements with no further treatment.

The intention of experimenting with thick woollen threads in this manner is to attempt to reproduce a fabric which has a more delicate appearance than the thread might indicate. The diamond-shaped blocks would be much more closely woven and more solid in appearance if worked in the normal manner in cloth-stitch or even half-stitch. By working the background netting in Dieppe Ground, the solid areas of work made by passing the threads from the ground directly across one another in whole stitch, are separated by relatively firm sections. The spiders are introduced to give a new dimension of oval shapes to the finished design. It is essential to make a very simple design for this type of thread, not only because it has a variegated colour scheme of pink and blue, but any fancy stitchery would be lost in the fluffiness of the fibres.

Only half of the pattern is given in the pricking, but it should be a relatively simple

Pricking 34. *'Spiders and Diamonds', a scarf in double knitting wool (half of width)*

1 Pattern Repeat

Fig. 36. *Alison and Amanda wearing their woollen bobbin lace scarves*

task to add a mirror image of itself to produce the final pattern with the correct width. Two rows of cloth stitch are worked across all the threads at the beginning and end of the work to make neat ends.

White scarf

This has far more detail than the one worked in double knitting wool. The thread used is the fine acrylic yarn sold for use with knitting machines. Its thickness is equivalent to 3-ply wool when doubled up. As can be seen in

Pricking 35. *White scarf in fine acrylic yarn*

Pricking 35, a far more intricate pattern can be worked with this finer thread to produce a lightweight, delicate fabric. There is very little shrinkage when using this yarn and the finished product launders well, although I would not recommend the use of a washing machine!

The design is based on two spiral shapes twisting in opposite directions. The working of alternate sections in whole stitch and half stitch helps to foster the illusion of continuous twisted ribbons flowing along the length of the scarf. By using honeycomb stitch for the background, it becomes more open in texture, providing a foil for the main features.

13 · Flowers

No volume which discusses lace design would be complete without a section devoted to lace flowers. Indeed, all lace forms depict these in some way or other and most incorporate floral shapes that are peculiar to that type of lace alone. Flowers have always been an integral part of lace patterns and designers through the centuries have let their imaginations run riot to produce some beautiful, intricate and realistic representations in their work. Although there are variations within each type, all our traditional laces are bound by certain rules and regulations which govern the scope, shape and range of the flowers which can be incorporated within their designs.

Bruges Flower Work even has the word 'flower' in its title. There are two major variations within this type of lace; the more recently evolved sort worked in thicker threads with a less intricate construction and the traditional fine Bruges Flower Work which has been made for some centuries, and is closely allied to Duchesse lace. All the designs worked in these techniques have flowers, leaves, scrolled stems and tendrils incorporated within them. In fact, one could say that there are no other design elements within any true Bruges Flower Work except for the filling stitches which bind these shapes into a whole.

The majority of Honiton lace designs are also of flowers and leaves, although animals and birds are featured in many forms. The flowers for this type of lace, though, are usually far more realistic then the stylized ones of the Bruges Flower Work, and are mostly asymmetrical in design rather than full-faced. Fronds of ferns are also a regular feature in Honiton lace patterns.

In Bucks Point lace many different flowers are represented in the designs. Indeed, some of the more intricate patterns are called 'Floral Bucks' and the majority of these are traditionally named after the flowers which they depict.

In the Beds/Maltese/Cluny family of laces most of the flowers consist of tallied petals in varying numbers which are daisy-like in appearance. This is in contrast to those laces which attempt a photographic representation of a number of different flowers. Some of the very intricate antique laces, however, do have some very realistic flowers and leaves within their designs. The patterns drawn by Thomas Lester, for example, illustrate this very clearly.

Even the more recently developed Schneeberg lace designs rely upon flowers for much of their inspiration, and certainly all the needle-made laces have always depended upon flowers for their designs. So where does this leave us? There seems to have been such a comprehensive interpretation of flowers and leaves already that it is very difficult for a modern designer to develop new ideas. Even the concept of three-dimensional flowers is not new. In the Museum of Royal History and Art in Brussels, there is a beautiful three-dimensional spray of flowers worked in Alençon needle lace which was made in France in the nineteenth century. Although this spray is made using all-white threads, coloured lace flowers have been incorporated into laces from their very beginnings. Colour and three-dimensions are not modern concepts at all, it seems.

Perhaps there is no way in which we can discover new interpretations! As the old saying goes, 'There is nothing new under the sun'. If we are to keep lace design alive, though, we must attempt to discover different ways of depicting flowers, if only because of the important part they have always played in the development of

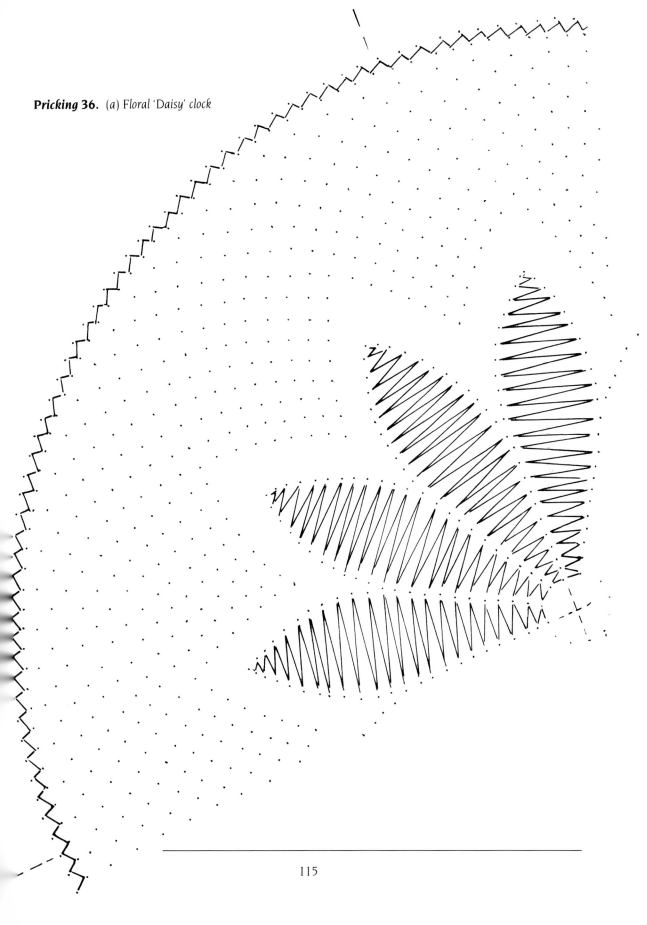

Pricking 36. (a) Floral 'Daisy' clock

design. The following two ways of tackling this problem may assist another designer to develop further lines of thought and methods of interpreting floral shapes.

Floral clock

This is an attempt to develop a slightly novel method of displaying a floral lace. The daisy is one of our more recognizable flower forms. It ranges from the tiny white variety that grows unwanted in our lawns to the large yellow sunflowers which reach many feet upwards and supply us with necessary oils. This floral clock is largely symbolic, incorporating time and the life-giving rays of the sun, with the familiar daisy shape representing plant-life vital to all life on earth.

Referring to pricking 36, it can be seen that the petals of the flower radiate from a central point together with the hands of the clock to form an integrated whole. The number and size of the petals could be adapted to suit other designs. When considering the actual clock numbers, they would not stand out with sufficient clarity if every one were to be worked as a number, but would take up too much space for accurate time-reading and the daisy decoration would be swamped. Therefore only the hour, quarters and half-hour are worked in actual numbers. The intervening ones are merely indicated by a single line. The thread used is 20 crochet cotton in the realistic colours of yellow and white for the flower with a white background netting to join the flower and black numbers together. With the advent of battery-

Fig. 37.
Floral 'Daisy' Clock

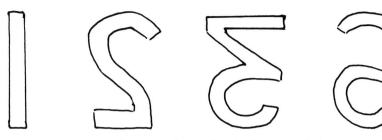

Pricking 36. (*b*) *Numbers for the 'Daisy' clock*

operated clock mechanisms, it is relatively easy to obtain the working parts for the clock. All that is needed then is a friendly wood-worker to make the background frame to contain the works, and to which the finished lace design is attached.

Three-dimensional flowers

Designing and making a flower arrangement similar to the one shown in figure 39 can prove to be a very interesting project. Similarly, a wedding bouquet constructed from lace flowers could be a beautiful and permanent souvenir of a happy occasion. In this way, too, the crafts of floristry and flower arranging can be used together with lacemaking. The actual flowers can be as realistic or imaginative as you please, and there is no need to worry about the flowering season and availability of the plants you will depict. Snowdrops and daffodils can be made and used together with roses or dahlias to form an effective blend of seasons. The variety of petal shapes and textures is immense and, of course, the colour (or not) can be chosen to match exactly other accessories and clothes where, in nature, this is not always possible.

Designing three-dimensional lacy flowers

Designing a life-like flower can be achieved by studying the structure and shape of a true flower, and then drawing each petal exactly to size and constructing the finished petals as realistically as possible. The following instructions are just for lacy flowers and can be adapted to suit any number of petal shape variations. If required, a design can consist of several layers of petals worked in this fashion to form a composite flower.

1 Draw a petal shape (see diagram 23*a*). If this proves difficult to do free-hand, draw round a real petal or use a template shape like those used by the makers of silk or paper flowers.

2 Repeat this petal as many times as required by tracing it or using a photocopier and position in a circular formation (see diagram 23*b*).

3 Now draw curved connecting lines between each petal as shown in diagram 23*c* to make a single continuous line round the entire shape. Make sure that this line is commenced a little way from the base of each petal shape.

4 One of three alternatives can now be chosen according to whichever method of making the flower is to be employed: (i) a narrow braid line can be marked if the flower is to be worked with an edge braid and a separate filling stitch; (ii) a wide braid line can be drawn if there is to be no other filling; and (iii) a single centre line is made if the flower is to be worked with solid cloth stitch or half stitch petals (see diagram 23*d, e,* and *f*).

5 The pin-hole positions can now be marked following the method used in the section for braid laces.

Methods of working three-dimensional flowers

There are a variety of different methods of working a flower in this manner and the one which will be used will have been decided upon before drawing it. By designing and working flowers as a continuous braid, with or without filling stitches, there are fewer ends of thread to conceal when it is made up. The braid must be commenced at the centre of the flower (at the base of a petal) and then the ends can be sewn in to their starting place as in normal braid

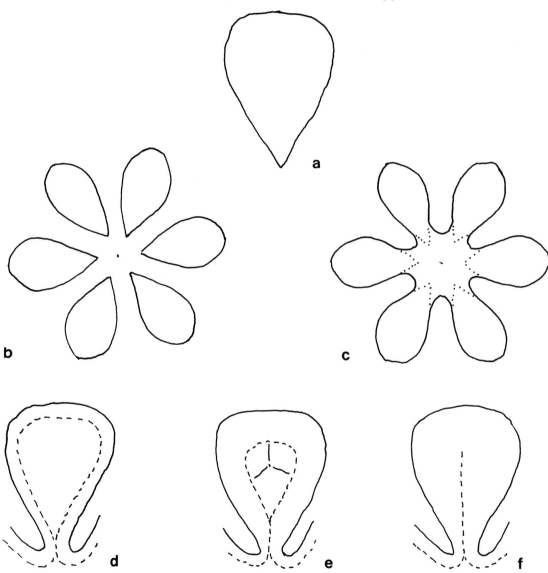

Diag. 23. *Drawing a three-dimensional flower design*

laces. It is not necessary or even desirable to cut these threads short. They can be bound together with the wire ends when forming the flower. There is usually a small empty circular space in the centre of the petalled shape.

Stiffening the flowers is dealt with a little later on but, at this stage, I must make mention of wiring the petals. If the petals are wired at their centre, each will have its own individual wire and these ends will be used for the stem. Similarly, if the edges of the petals are to be wired, it is preferable to use a separate piece of wire for each petal (leaving the two ends for

each petal). Do not take a single piece of wire round the entire shape. If you do this, the centre becomes too rigid and bulky and the flower will not have a neat shape at this point. Remember that it is better, whenever possible, to work the wire in conjunction with the lace, rather than to sew it on afterwards, as it is more secure and less likely to come adrift.

Diagram 24 shows some of the various methods and direction of work for these flowers. Within each there is scope for adaptation and improvisation, so only a few general remarks are needed.

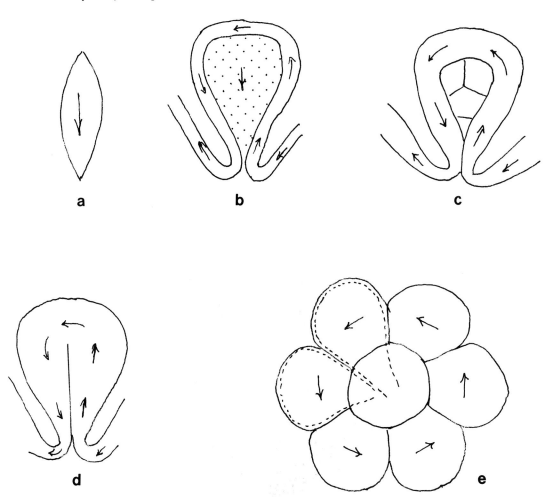

Diag. 24. *Working directions for three-dimensional flowers*

(a) This is the shape of a petal that is best worked from the top to the base. Each is made independently of the others and any number can be used for a flower of the daisy-type.

(b) Here we have a narrow braid worked continuously round all the petals with the centre of each requiring a filling stitch of some sort. Tulle du Puy, Dieppe Ground, Rose Ground and Honeycomb Ground are amongst those which are very effective.

(c) This is worked in a similar fashion to (**b**) but, in this instance, the braid widens as it forms the petal shape. More bobbins can be used to accommodate this but it is better to change from whole stitch to whole stitch and twist as this makes a more delicate lace. The filling which unites the edge is merely false plaits or twisted pairs and is worked at the same time as the braid, using its worker threads.

(d) Each petal consists entirely of the braid,

Fig. 38. *Three flowers – each is made by a different method: (a) narrow braid with a filling stitch, (b) wide braid with no separate filling, (c) each petal is made independently*

with the second half attached by sewings to the part already worked. Half-stitch is very useful here and a pivot pin (as used in Bruges Flower Work) is worked at the top of the central vein.

(e) This flower is worked in the same way as a Bruges flower. It looks most effective with every petal made in half-stitch. Each petal is wired whilst it is being made and the dotted line on the diagram indicates the position of two of these wires.

In figure 38 we can see three flowers, each of which has been made by a different method. The large flower arrangement consists of flowers made by these and other methods and all the leaves are also worked in lace.

Stiffening three-dimensional flowers

As the petals of the flowers described above are worked in a relatively open-work lace, some form of stiffening is required. If a flower is made entirely in cloth stitch and is an exact replica of a real one, the built-in stiffness and its assemblage should normally be sufficient for it to hold its shape with no external aids. As these are just lacey flowers, however, they have very little of this intrinsic stiffness and need some form of artificial assistance. There is only one recommended method of providing this help without distorting the lace or damaging and discolouring the thread, and that is the discreet use of wire.

The two main traditional methods of using starch or sugar water to give extra body to lace have some major problems for stiffening this type of work. If they are used on lace which is to be laundered and then restiffened, they have their uses, but, remember, these flowers are to be left *in situ* for (hopefully) a number of years without requiring any further attention and, therefore, need to be treated with great care. One of the two chief problems associated with starch and sugar water is that they both lose

Fig. 39. A Flower Arrangement – *every flower and leaf is made in lace – only the mimosa balls are machine-made. The overall size of the frame is 16" by 20"*

their stiffening properties when encountering a high atmospheric humidity, and the lace which has been treated solely in this manner becomes extremely limp. The arrangement soon loses its shape and it becomes almost impossible to restore it to its original appearance. The second problem, with sugar water in particular, is that because the rigidity is formed by several applications, it adds a thick coating to the thread. This makes the lace appear clumsy and it loses its original delicate appearance. It also becomes discoloured after a time and, as with starch, the thread could be damaged by long-term contact.

It is far better to provide any extra stiffening by the discreet use of rust-proof wire. This should be the type of brass wire used for spangling bobbins, fuse wire, or millinery wire. There is also a silvery-grey soft wire which can be purchased from craft shops and this is suitable, but florist's wire can become rusty and is not really recommended. Millinery wire is made in a variety of thicknesses and is coated with a cotton substance which can be coloured with felt-tip pens or cold water dyes to match the thread used to make the flower. If desired, other wire can be tightly bound with the same thread which made the flower so that it remains invisible. If wire cannot be woven into the petal during its construction, it should be sewn on the reverse side afterwards using the same thread that made the flower. Do *not* attach wire to the lace flower by the use of any type of adhesive. However 'invisible' and 'safe' a glue may be advertised to be, there is always a possibility that at some future date it could cause damage to the thread either by discolouration or by causing it to disintegrate.

The wire may either be positioned as a central vein for each petal or used to stiffen the edge by working it together with the outside passive threads. The actual method used depends on how the flower is constructed. Consideration must also be given as to whether there is sufficient thread in the centre of each petal to support the wire, or if it would be less visible round the edge. Remember, once again, these are not real flowers!

The same criteria apply to leaves. Both leaves and petals, when treated in this manner, have a certain malleability. Other methods of providing extra stiffening such as hair lacquer, or, in a dire emergency, clear nail varnish, should *never* be used for long-term permanency. If the flower does not retain its shape using wire and its own built-in tension, you might as well discard it and start again using a different thread, or more bobbins, or adjust the pattern accordingly.

Assembling three-dimensional flowers

Once the petals are made and wired, it is a relatively simple task to finish the flower. Realistic stamens can be purchased from many craft shops or tiny beads can be used. A small bundle of these are firmly attached to another piece of wire which is then threaded through the centre hole of the flower so that the stamens are on the right side of the lace. The flower is then gathered together at the base of the petals with the stamens in the middle. The wires and thread ends can be twisted to form a stem which is then bound with florists' tape. Now bend and position the petals to form the flower shape required.

Flowers made in this manner can look most attractive when used as a spray corsage or even just a single flower, with or without leaves. A small safety pin is sewn to the stem and the leaf or leaf spray is added to disguise this.

14 · Lace from lace

As the various methods of producing lace have evolved, so the designs have developed along parallel lines. The very first laces which came about from cut work and drawn thread work to become Punto in Ario gave rise to some of the original guipure bobbin laces, which imitated the straight narrow lines of the needle-made lace.

As the design for one type of lace changed according to fashion and the inventiveness of the designers, so the other forms also altered, with the shapes of the patterns retaining remarkable similarity. This has meant that pieces of lace with like designs could be made using more than one technique, and we find numerous examples of, say, a needle-made centre design with bobbin or crochet edges. Other sectional laces became accepted with more detailed sections worked in needlepoint, the general or less detailed parts being made by bobbins and pillow.

It is rarely possible and never desirable to create an identical lace from one originally worked by a different method. The very fact that construction methods are so varied precludes this, but an interesting exercise can be worked to reproduce a new design with very similar shapes to a piece of lace made in another medium. It is also possible to isolate small areas of an antique lace and make modern versions of them.

In this section we are going to examine several different possibilities. Once the basic procedures for these are learnt, the designer can explore other avenues and do her own research into the possibilities of expansion. On occasion it will be found that the shapes produced by working a single-thread type of lace cannot be formed satisfactorily using multi-thread techniques. If this happens, the attempt should be abandoned and further research must be done to seek a more suitable design to work upon.

The main problem with making designs for bobbin laces which are similar to single-thread laces is that the single thread performs in a different fashion from a collection of threads. Therefore, for example, the edge of a crochet mat is not constructed in the same manner as one made in bobbin lace. When working a knitted lace mat, though, it is quite normal to crochet a pointed chain-stitch edge which unites the stitches from the knitting needle into small groups. This is a relatively similar effect to a bobbin lace plaited nine-pin edge and the shape can be translated from one medium to the other with ease.

Thistle motif

Most of our antique laces have beautiful shapes within their designs. It would be ludicrous to attempt to reproduce them exactly as they stand without using the correct thread (which is now unavailable) or having the precise knowledge which went into their creation, but it makes a worthwhile experiment to select a single shape from their midst and attempt the design of a 'modern' variation.

The thistle motif was initiated and inspired by a lovely antique collar in the reserve collection at Luton Museum. Figure 40 shows a close-up section of this collar in which its construction is clearly visible. This particular piece of lace has added interest because the various motifs which form its make-up are produced by a combination of both bobbin and needlepoint techniques. Mrs Doreen Fudge, the

◆

Keeper of Art at the museum, assures me that this particular collar is known as 'Bastard' lace. It can be seen clearly in the photograph that the thistles are made in bobbin lace but that their leaves are formed with needle and thread. This combination of motifs made by two different techniques, all joined together by bobbin-made brides or bars with picots, has produced a delicately textured piece of work which is well balanced and impossible to reproduce nowadays.

By examining the construction of the thistle heads, it is possible to design similar ones

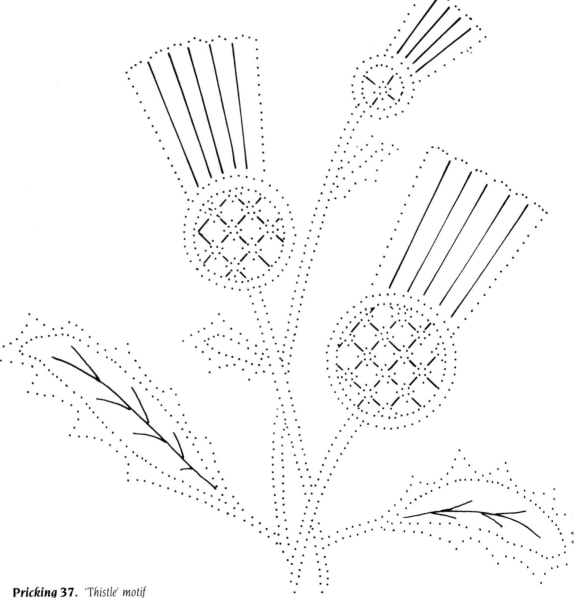

Pricking 37. *'Thistle' motif*

Fig. 40. *Enlargement of a section of the antique collar which inspired the 'Thistle' design – this is part of the lace collection at Luton Museum*

which have the same shape and appearance as the original version. Therefore, by drawing a comparable shape, a new interpretation can be produced which is shown in pricking 37. The two versions can be compared by looking at figures 40 and 42. The arrangement of the flower heads on the collar is not suitable for exact reproduction so, rather than draw only one single flower which would give the appearance of an unfinished end product, a small group can be made, adding some leaves and stems to complete the design. This makes a neat formation with plenty of space around each

separate thistle, thus producing an attractive picture. DMC Brillante d'Alsace 30 thread was used to make the lace in the naturalistic colours of purple and green. This helps to give the work a little more realism.

The original needle-made leaves have prominent veins, so this version should also indicate these. They have been embroidered in chain-stitch directly on to the backing material after the lace was mounted. Of course, they could have been worked in ten-stick, pin-chain or as plaits, but these methods would have meant extra-careful treatment of the lace when

Fig. 41. *Three different lace forms – knitted, crochet and mixed bobbin and needlepoint*

◆

Fig. 42. Bobbin made 'modern' versions of the items in Fig. 41

mounting it to ensure that they were positioned correctly. Another method of depicting the leaves would have been to work the entire leaf in lace, and not just the edges. Then the veins could have been indicated by the use of a thick gimp thread.

When wishing to complete similar exercises from other antique laces, the assistance of a good magnifying glass is absolutely essential. In this way, the original stitches used can be determined and reproduced as accurately as possible in their new setting. For a first attempt, a suitable flower would be the carnation. This has always been very popular amongst designers of all types of lace and has appeared with great regularity in many lace forms throughout the ages. This means that there are many more opportunities to discover a suitable example from which to work.

Round mat

When attempting to translate the shapes produced by working another type of lace into bobbin lace, a somewhat more complicated procedure is necessary. As well as showing the 'thistle' lace, figures 41 and 42 also depict knitted and crocheted lace with their bobbin-made versions. The pricking for the round mat which imitates the crocheted one is given (pricking 38).

Two different threads have been used for this design. The inner section requires 42 pairs of bobbins and BOUC Fil de Lin 50 thread whilst the outer part needs 22 pairs with Bockens 35 linen thread.

Whatever the method used to make the original lace, it is always preferable for the designer to have made it herself. This is not essential but it does give a prior insight into its construction and frequently the future possibilities can be considered whilst it is in the process of being worked. The following instructions give one method of translating

knitted or crocheted patterns into bobbin lace designs. No doubt, there are other ways of doing this and each designer will find her own variations.

1 Pin out the original piece of lace on a flat, even surface. Try to ensure the accuracy of this and that it is made as square, round, octagonal etc. as possible. Use a tape measure to check this because precision at this stage makes the designing of the bobbin lace version much easier.

2 Place a piece of tracing paper on the pinned-out original and trace the main structure lines and shapes. The outline, of course, must be drawn first and then the dominant shapes and any other inner structural lines which need to be included. When reproducing a large piece of lace, it should be sufficient merely to work upon a quarter or just one section of the piece. Check on the number of pattern repeats. Many round crochet mats have seven repeats. This means that to obtain the accuracy needed for the bobbin version, polar graph paper is required, and seven does not go exactly into 360° upon which it is based. A certain amount of 'fiddling' is then required. Frequently, it proves impossible to use and not worth the effort involved, so it may be worthwhile to check on the number of pattern repeats before commencing, and ensure its suitability first.

3 Having obtained the rough outline, the tracing paper can be removed and transferred on to a piece of graph paper in order to commence work on the design. Keep the original piece of lace pinned out until this is complete, so that frequent checks can be made to compare the two versions.

4 The lines that have been traced will not be absolutely accurate so, using the graph paper lines, make them true and re-draw them in their

Pricking 38. *Round mat design*
(quarter of pattern)

required positions. Make sure, also, that the outside edge is a smooth even shape.

5 Commencing with a dominant feature of the design, (for example, a major shape which will require cloth stitch to work it) assess the possibilities as to how it will be worked. The places where the threads will enter and leave when it has been completed must be determined. The original lace can help here by providing a starting point, but a certain amount of adaptation will probably be required.

6 Now the secondary shapes and areas of background filling between the dominant parts can be drawn, indicating the paths the threads will follow rather than actual pin positions, so that a working diagram can be produced. In this manner, any parts where the threads cannot be transversed in a logical, smooth progression should be adapted and altered to accommodate the different techniques required from the original method of construction.

7 Finally, once a really accurate working diagram has been completed, the approximate pin-hole positions can be indicated and the required thread determined upon. The section which has been completed can be reproduced as many times as required and the final pricking of the whole design can be assembled ready for use.

Tape lace conversions

When wishing to make a bobbin lace design from a piece of tape lace (Branscombe Point, Renaissance type, etc.) or even from a needlepoint original, the main problem encountered is discovering a piece where the tape outline is continuous. A machine-made tape with needle-made fillings is rarely used uncut throughout the entire design. The tape is frequently either folded on top of itself to continue to the next section or severed and recommenced at a different place. Therefore, many of these laces are not really suitable for translation into bobbin lace designs. Working a bobbin braid lace in this manner is cumbersome and rather untidy with a large number of places which have cut ends to conceal. This is fine when working such laces as Bruges Flower Work where the sections are specifically designed to be thus worked. Other sectional laces are more allied to Russian Tape lace patterns where the braid is of a constant width and is worked as a continuous piece with no stops and starts. Another flaw is that each joining place is a weak spot and can come adrift with use.

If, however, you do discover a pattern that is adaptable for translation into bobbin lace, the shapes of the needle-made fillings can frequently be reconstructed with bobbin-made look-alikes and the two pieces of lace can look remarkably similar.

True 'lace from lace'

There is another possibility where a pattern can be made from an existing piece of bobbin lace when the original pricking is not in your possession. This particular exercise is of great value in the assessment of your own work standards and in the understanding of the structure of certain types of 'free' lace. The best pieces to use as examples, in order to introduce yourself to this type of work, are those purchased in other countries. They are usually of fairly coarse construction which is readily visible even to those of us with poor eyesight. Many a time the cry of 'I could do that pattern' is heard when friends bring back their souvenirs, and the following technique may help you to do just that. A word of warning, though. Do *not* pass the pricking so made to any other person. This must remain for your sole use in order to prevent an infringement of any copyright that may be in existence on the original design. Figure 43 shows a mat made in this manner together with the purchased one. (The bought lace is at the top!)

The first step is to pin out the lace as near as possible to its correct shape, in the same way as for the round mat. In this instance, though, a piece of stiff white card must be placed under the lace and on top of a flat piece of polystyrene which is used as the base. Commencing at the centre of the piece of lace, re-position the pins in their original places and work outwards towards the outside edge. The lace can usually be stretched considerably and frequently ends up nearly double its apparent size. When the whole piece of lace has been so stretched, there should be a pin in every place where there was one whilst it was being constructed. It should now be possible to see where the worker threads have travelled, and the passage of other threads throughout the whole piece. Make sure that the first time you attempt this procedure, the lace is not too large and the construction is fairly simple with reasonably thick threads, otherwise a magnifying glass will be required!

The lace can now be removed from the card by taking out all the pins. In order to prevent it from shrinking back to its former size, it can be treated with a little spray starch or unperfumed hair lacquer before removing the pins. This helps to prevent it from shrinking again whilst you are working on the design.

The resulting pin-holes in the white card which was under the lace can now be used as a basis of preparing the final pricking. These holes are rarely absolutely accurate and nearly always require further adjustment. Most of those that should be in a straight line are not and the use of a pencil and ruler is necessary to ensure their accuracy. The working lines can now be drawn making use of the original piece

Fig. 43. *'Lace from lace' – the original purchased in Belgium and the copy made from the original by myself*

of lace as a reference. Check that any section that should be circular or square is also correct and has not become some other odd shape!

Once the working lines and trued-up holes are marked, the card can be used as a preliminary pricking. Rather than spending a long time making an actual pricking, the new lace can be made using the drawing just prepared on top of a fresh piece of white card. This means the two pieces of card, one on top of the other, are used as a base. The underneath piece will act as the final pricking after the new lace has been made. The correct working lines can be drawn in black fine-line pen and the design on the card photocopied. The holes will be reproduced as black dots and an excellent pattern is the result.

15 · Beads and Sequins

Queen Elizabeth I used to bedeck herself with lace which was frequently adorned with seed pearls and other jewels. This fashion was gradually abandoned with the advent of monarchs who dressed more soberly and it has never since reached the heights it once attained.

There is definitely a case for resurrecting this decoration of lace, although real jewels are, of course, completely out of the reach of most of us. We have to make do with ordinary mass-produced beads and sequins of various colours and shapes. Perhaps this is all to the good as real jewels are much heavier than their plastic and man-made look-alikes and, therefore, the lace they adorn needs to be of heavier construction and requires a lot of stiffening to prevent the distortion of its shape.

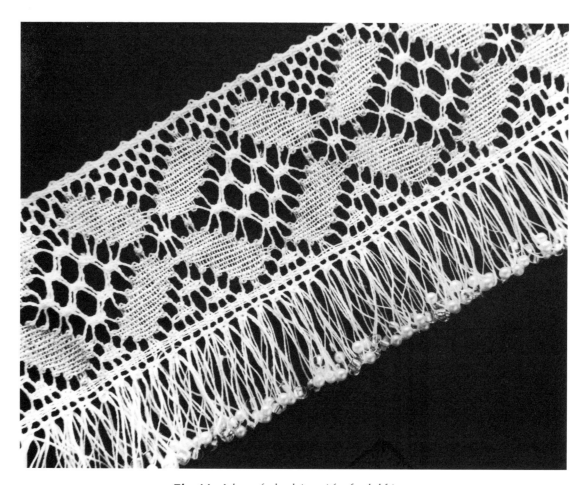

Fig. 44. *A lampshade edging with a beaded fringe*

Figures 44, 45 and 46 show a few of the ways in which beads can be attached to lace in order not only to adorn the design, but also to help to bring it alive. For instance, a faceted red sequin, used as the eye of a golden dragon, will give it that spark of life which makes all the difference between a piece of lace which is merely 'pretty', and one which is transformed into a work of art. Some ideas for the use of sequins and beads are listed below and perhaps these will assist another designer to discover more ways of using them to decorate her own work.

1 One of the most obvious ways of using beads is to give weight to fringing. Just as lead weights are placed in hems to keep the bottoms of curtains, coats and skirts in their correct place and to help them 'hang' better, so a small bead at the bottom of a free-hanging loop of thread

Fig. 45. *Traditional Bucks Point, Beds/Maltese and Torchon edgings with added beads at the headsides*

will give it a better 'set'. The fringing on the 'windmill' edge design is shown in figure 44. This piece of lace was designed for use as a lampshade decoration. When using beads for this type of work, it is worthwhile remembering that glass (or clear plastic) beads will reflect the light from the lamp and produce a lovely sparkle that would be missing from matt or opaque beads. In order to make this type of fringe thick enough, the pair of bobbins required must have at least two independent threads wound on them, each of which is strung separately with beads. Alternatively, two pairs of bobbins, each wound with a single thread, can be worked together as one pair. If a fuller effect is required, three pairs of bobbins can be used as a single pair, but this number can sometimes be a little unwieldy to work evenly. A long knot-free length of thread is required to work a fringe and the beads must all be strung on before winding the bobbins. Therefore, the use of large continental-type bobbins is recommended. Note that it will be necessary to ensure that the beaded part of the thread is wound round the shank of the bobbins as well as the neck.

2 A natural progression from the lampshade fringing is the use of a string of beads as shown in the top sample in figure 45. The design used for this particular example is a Bucks Point pattern called 'String of Pearls', which can be found in 100 *Traditional Bobbin Lace Patterns* by Geraldine Stott and Bridget M. Cook (see Further Reading list). This pattern lends itself admirably to the use of a string of pearlized beads draped along the head side instead of the traditional edge. This type of work looks very attractive when attached to the edge of a dress yoke or collar. It could also be used by itself as a choker by attaching a ring and loop at each end. Once again, the beads are strung on to the thread before the bobbin is wound, but only one bobbin is required on this occasion and it

Fig. 46. Beads and sequins decorating lace in various ways

is advisable to use a thick thread for this. Allowance has then been made for the weight of the beads which could break a finer thread. Imagine the havoc caused if it snapped whilst the lace was being worn!

3 Further ways of displaying beads at the head side of a piece of lace can be seen in the other edgings in figure 45. In these instances, the beads are not put on the thread beforehand but attached whilst the lace is being made, by working sewings with the worker pair instead of working a picot or normal edge pin. Diagram 25 shows how this can be done. The photograph shows how effective this use of beads can be on Bucks Point, Beds/Maltese and Torchon laces. Sometimes it is better not to use every pin-hole to attach the beads but to use every other one, or merely selective ones. It must be left to the discretion of the lacemaker to decide for herself the way in which they will be shown to most advantage.

4 The little mouse in figure 46 shows how a small round bead can be used most effectively as an eye. Although the working of animals' eyes was discussed earlier, the difficulty of producing perfectly formed round eyes was not mentioned. It is virtually impossible to produce an ideal tiny circle and a better, more accurate end product can be achieved by the use of a bead rather than a poorly-made tally. In this instance, the bead is sewn on separately to the right side after the lace has been taken off the pillow. In a similar way, the pupils of an owl's eyes can be depicted by the use of beads or sequins which are added afterwards. Try positioning them in several places before finally attaching them, as the bird's expression can change considerably according to their size and placement. A bead can also replace a small raised tally in the centre of a section of cloth stitch or half-stitch in a piece of Beds/Maltese lace. This is again attached by working a sewing.

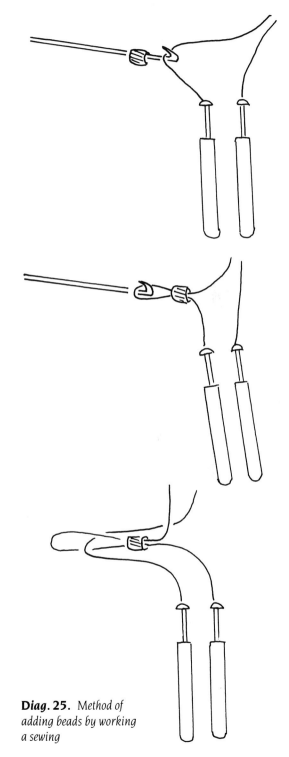

Diag. 25. *Method of adding beads by working a sewing*

5 The little spruce tree (figure 46) has a few beads suitably positioned to help create the effect of the drooping branches of that type of tree. In real life, the shape of the branches has a lovely swathing effect. This is quite difficult to reproduce faithfully in lace so it is better merely to indicate this downward movement in a few relevant places. Once again, the beads are attached by working sewings with the worker threads whilst the lace is being made.

6 The tiny earrings have a small pearl bead sewn on (like the mouse's eye) after the lace is completed. Their purpose here is not only decorative but, as the earrings are so small and lightweight, they also disguise some of the thread ends and add weight to enable them to hang correctly, too.

7 The abstract design 'Spirit of Freedom' demonstrates the use of beads and sequins together in one piece, and three different methods of attaching them.
(i) The entire edge of the two main sections of the design consists of a string of pearls. These are strung on the outside passive bobbin which is wound with a thicker thread and used as a gimp. One bead is then released between each pin-hole.
(ii) The large area of beads in the centre is made by working a sewing with two pairs of bobbins instead of a pin at each of the places where the threads normally cross. In this manner a solid shape can be formed. If beads of various colours were to be used in this way, an attractive colourful pattern could be formed.
(iii) The sequins (with bead centres) are sewn on afterwards. A gimp thread is woven into the lace whilst it is in the process of being made to mark the position of this curved line of sequins and to strengthen the lace at that point ready for their attachment. The two small motifs on the bottom section are also worked in this manner but a gimp thread is unnecessary here.

8 Another form of adornment can be seen on the braid lace motif in figure 46. Here the beads are strung on to a centre passive bobbin, used as a gimp, and one is released at regular intervals. The finished effect is very attractive and numerous colour combinations can be made. One thing to remember when working in this manner, though, is that the right side of the work is uppermost and not facing the pillow as normal. This means that any knots in the thread must be positioned underneath the work in hand instead of being brought to the surface. Also, when joining the braid's start to its finish, once the sewings have been made, the threads are cut *long* and woven to the back of the braid in order to make them invisible. They are then ready to be tied and finished after the lace has been taken off the pillow.

These few examples of the use of beads and sequins are but the tip of an iceberg and have been kept simple deliberately. Once colour is introduced, a great number of realistic designs can be worked. Red beads can be used as berries with green lace leaves; the jewels on a crown can be indicated in various colours; or the black dots on ermine fur can be shown. Cylindrical bugle beads make excellent toggles for duffle coats or strands of green ones could make centre veins for leaves. The list is endless and many designs can be enhanced in this way.

16 · 'Dot-to-dot' design

Dot-to-dot – a game played by us all at some stage of our lives. Where its origins lie no one knows, but it is one of the oldest games in the world. Perhaps the most well-known results are to be seen in the world of Astronomy. The stars in the night sky acted as the dots for the astronomers of the ancient world when they inspired the shapes of the Great Bear, The Archer, Pegasus and all the other constellations. These have become the signs of the zodiac which are used by the astrologers who cast our horoscopes. It takes a considerable amount of imagination to recognize most of these shapes, made by drawing imaginary lines from one star in a group to another. The important factor for designers is that it gives an insight into the possibilities of making distinguishable shapes in this manner.

Therefore, a scaled-down version of this game can be used to heighten a designer's awareness of line, shape, space and texture. Many people complain that they cannot draw, but everybody can join two dots on a piece of paper with a line, however straight or wavering it may be! The results can be most illuminating and very rewarding.

The tools required for this 'game' are extremely simple – a sheet of plain white paper, pencil, eraser and a few grains of rice, lentils, currants, etc.. The method of playing is as follows:-

1 Place the sheet of paper flat on a table. Hold about twenty or so grains between your thumb and forefinger and release them about six inches above the paper, so that they drop directly on to it.

2 Mark a dot at each place where a grain has fallen and then remove the grains. (It is *not* a good idea to cook and eat them now!)

3 Next draw a continuous line from one dot to its neighbour. In the first instance, use only the ones that form an outline which will enclose all the others. Frequently, this shape resembles an object, although rarely in its exact shape.

4 Now join the internal dots together in groups. Quite often, several will be formed into obvious shapes or even sets of parallel curved lines. This produces further secondary structures. If there was no obvious design to be seen when the outside dots were joined, by uniting these inner ones, a clue may well be given or a form may even appear, and the outer dots can then be ignored.

5 It is now a logical progression to erase any of the lines which appear incongruous and do not fit in with the others. The same applies to any dot which is superfluous. Not every grouping of dots is suitable, so, if no shape appears at first, lay that design to one side and start again from the beginning.

Gradually the memory is trained to recognise certain groupings and the fact that adjacent to one set of dots may be another that follows similar lines and which provides the necessary hint. In this way, either an abstract or true-to-life design with complementary sets of inner lines will begin to emerge.

6 Now is the time to use artistic licence and to adjust the lines which join the dots, in order to produce smoother curves which are compatible with one another. Lines can be drawn near dots instead of through them and it is not necessary to end a line at a dot: it can be extended to finish at any required place.

7 Once an outline of a shape is formed with satisfactory internal lines, the method of working it and the stitches and threads to be used can be determined. The design 'Spirit of Freedom' shown in figure 46 was evolved in this manner. Several other shapes with their original dot marks can be seen in diagrams 26 to 29. The original dots have been left so that it can be seen how the lines have been adapted to form the final designs.

This exercise is really excellent in assisting with development of the senses and it enables a designer to improve her skills in the art of drawing and shape recognition. Never say that you cannot draw. Any person who can hold a pencil can draw a line. After that, it is just a matter of practice and learning to appreciate the qualities required to make that line into the basis of a design which will produce balanced, attractive 'modern' lace.

And so my wish for you all is, happy lacemaking and enjoy your designing!

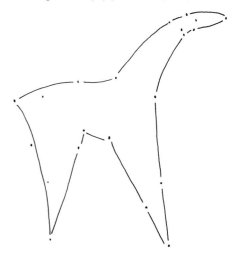

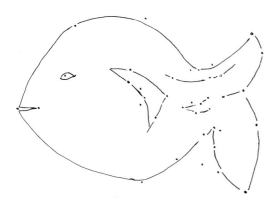

Diag. 26. *'Fish' design obtained by the 'dot-to-dot' method*

Diag. 27. *'Prehistoric Cave Drawing' design*

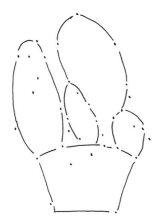

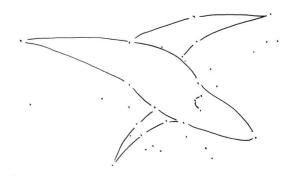

Diag. 28. *Drawing for a design of 'Cactii in a Pot'*

Diag. 29. *'Dolphin'*

Recommended FurtherReading

ATKINSON, Jane, *Pattern Design for Torchon Lace*, Batsford

BRIGGS, W, & Co, *Designs and Patterns for Embroiderers and craftsmen*

COLLIER, Ann, *Creative Design in Bobbin Lace*, Batsford

COLLIER, Ann, *New Designs in Bobbin Lace*, Batsford

COOK, Bridget, *Practical Skills in Bobbin Lace*, Batsford

COOK, Bridget and STOTT, Geraldine, *The Book of Bobbin Lace Stitches*, Batsford

COOK, Bridget and STOTT, Geraldine, *100 Traditional Bobbin Lace Patterns*, Batsford

EARNSHAW, Pat, *Lace in Fashion*, Batsford

GIERL, Irmgard, *Cross Stitch Patterns*, Batsford

LEVEY, Santina, *Lace: A History*, V & A Publications

REIGATE, Emily, *Illustrated Guide to Lace*, Antique Collectors Club

SORENSON, Veronica, *Modern Lace Designs*, Batsford

SPRINGETT, Christine, *Designing and Mounting Lace Fans*

SUTTON, Edna, *Designing for Bruges Flower Lace*, Dryad Press/ Batsford

WILLMOT, Joyce, *Lace Flowers*, Ruth Bean

The Book of Kells

List of Suppliers

For linen by the metre (yard) and made up articles of church linen:

Mary Collings
Church Furnishings
St Andrews Hall
Humber Doucy Lane
Ipswich
Suffolk
IP4 3BP

Hayes and Finch
Head Office and Factory
Hanson Road
Aintree
Liverpool
L9 7BP

General Suppliers:
United Kingdom
Alby-Lace Museum
Cromer Road
Alby
Norfolk
NR11 7QE

Bedford Lace
4 Newnham Street
Bedford

Campden Needlecraft
Centre
High Street
Chipping Campden
Gloucestershire

Chosen Crafts Centre
46 Winchcombe Street
Cheltenham
Gloucestershire
GL52 2ND

Leonie Cox
The Old School
Childswickham
Near Broadway
Worcs
WR12 7HD

Jo Firth
Lace Marketing and
Needlecraft Supplies
58 Kent Crescent
Lowtown
Pudsey
West Yorkshire
LS28 9EB

J. and J. Ford
October Hill
Upper Way
Upper Longdon
Rugeley
Staffordshire
WS15 1QB

Framecraft
83 Hampstead Road
Handsworth Wood
Birmingham
B2L 1JA

Mr R. Gravestock
Highwood
Crews Hill
Alfrick
Worcestershire
WR6 5HF

Hepatica
82a Water Lane
Wilmslow
Cheshire

Frank Herring & Sons
27 High West Street
Dorchester
Dorset
DT1 1UP

Honiton Lace Shop
44 High Street
Honiton
Devon

D.J. Hornsby
149 High Street
Burton Latimer
Kettering
Northants
NN15 5RL

and
25 Manwood Avenue
Canterbury
Kent
CT2 7AH

Pastimes
24–6 West Street
Alresford
Hampshire

Jane's Pincushion
Taverham Craft Unit 4
Taverham Nursery Centre
Fir Covert Road
Taverham
Norwich
NR8 6HT

All branches of John Lewis

Lambourn Valley Cottage
Industries
11 Oxford Street
Lambourn
Berks
RG16 7XS

Mace and Nairn
89 Crane Street
Salisbury
Wiltshire
SP1 2PY

Iris Martin
Farthing Cottage
Clickers Yard
Yardley Road
Olney
Bucks

Needlework
Ann Bartleet
Bucklers Farm
Coggeshall
Essex
CO6 1SB

The Needlewoman
21 Needles Alley
off New Street
Birmingham
B2 5AE

T. Parker
124 Corhampton Road
Boscombe East
Bournemouth
BH6 5NZ

Dorothy Pearce
5 Fulshaw Avenue
Wilmslow
Cheshire
SK9 51A

Jane Playford
North Lodge
Church Close
West Runton
Norfolk
NR27 9QY

Christine Riley
53 Barclay Street
Stonehaven
Kincardineshire
Scotland

Pat Savory
Tanglewood
4 Sanden Close
Hungerford
Berks
RG17 0LB

Peter and Beverley Scarlett
Strupak
Hill Head
Coldwells
Ellon, Grampian

Ken and Pat Schultz
134 Wisbech Road
Thornley
Peterborough

J.S. Sear
Lacecraft Supplies
8 Hill View
Sherrington
Buckinghamshire

Sebalace
Waterloo Mills
Howden Road
Silsden
W. Yorks
BD2 0HA

A. Sells
49 Pedley Lane
Clifton
Shefford
Bedfordshire

Shireburn Lace
Finkle Court
Finkle Hill
Sherburn in Elmet
N. Yorks
LS25 6EB

Stephen Simpson
Avenham Road Works
Preston
Lancs

Stiches
Dovehouse Shopping
Parade
Warwick Road
Olton
Solihull
West Midlands

S.M.P.
4 Garners Close
Chalfont St Peter
Bucks
SL9 0HB

Teazle Embroideries
35 Boothferry Road
Hull
North Humberside

Valley House Crafts
Studios
Ruston
Scarborough
N. Yorks

George Walker
The Corner Shop
Rickinghall
Diss
Norfolk

George White
40 Heath Drive
Boston Spa
LS23 6PB

Bobbins
A.R. Archer
The Poplars
Shelland
Near Stowmarket
Suffolk
IP14 3DE

T. Brown
Temple Lane Cottage
Littledean
Cinderford
Gloucestershire

Bridge Bookshop
7 Bridge Street
Bath
Avon
B82 4AS

Stephen Cook
'Cottage Crafts'
6 Woodland Close
Flackwell Heath
Buckinghamshire
HP10 9EP

Chrisken Bobbins
26 Cedar Drive
Kingsclere
Newbury
Bucks
RG15 8TD

Malcolm J. Fielding
2 Northern Terrace
Moss Lane
Silverdale
Lancs
LA5 0ST

Richard Gravestock
Highwood
Crews Hill
Alfrick
Worcestershire
WR6 5HF

Larkfield Crafts
Hilary Rickitts
4 Island Cottages
Mapledurwell
Basingstoke
Hants
RG25 2LU

Lambourn Valley Cottage
Industries
11 Oxford Street
Lambourn
Berks
RG16 7XS

T. Parker
124 Corhampton Road
Boscombe East
Bournemouth
BH6 5NZ

Bryn Phillips
'Pantglas'
Cellan
Lampeter
Dyfed
SA48 8JD

D.H. Shaw
47 Zamor Crescent
Thruscroft
Rotherham
S. Yorks
S66 9QD

Sizelands
1 Highfield Road
Winslow
Bucks
MK10 3QU

Spangler (Carole Morris)
1 Cashburn Lane
Burwell
Cambs
CB5 0ED

Christine and David
Springett
21 Hillmorton Road
Rugby
Warwickshire
CV22 5DF

Richard Viney
Unit 7
Port Royal Street
Southsea
Hants
PO5 4NP

Lace pillows
Newnham Lace Equipment
15 Marlowe Close
Basingstoke
Hants
RG24 9DD

Books
Christopher Williams
19 Morrison Avenue
Parkstone
Poole
Dorset
BH1Z 4AD

Silk embroidery and lace thread
E. and J. Piper
Silverlea
Flax Lane
Glemsford, Suffolk
CO10 7RS

Silk weaving yarn
Hilary Chetwynd
Kipping Cottage
Cheriton
Alresford
Hants
SO24 0PW

Frames and mounts
Doreen Campbell
'Highcliff'
Bremilham Road
Malmesbury
Wilts

Matt coloured transparent adhesive film
Heffers Graphic Shop
26 King Street
Cambridge
CB1 1LN

United States of America
Arbor House
22 Arbor Lane
Roslyn Hights
NY 11577

Baltazor Inc.
3262 Severn Avenue
Metairie
LA 7002

Beggars' Lane
P.O. Box 17263
Denver
Colorado 80217

Berga Ullman Inc.
P.O. Box 918
North Adams
Massachusetts 01247

Frederick J. Fawcett
129 South Street
Boston
Massachusetts 02130

Frivolite
15526 Densmore N.
Seattle
Washington 98113

Happy Hands
3007 S. W. Marshall
Pendleton
Oregon 97180

International Old Lacers
P.O. Box 1029
Westminster
Colorado 80030

Lace Place de Belgique
800 S. W. 17th Street
Boca Raton
FL 33432

Lacis
2150 Stuart Street
Berkeley
California 9470

Robin's Bobbins
RTL Box 1736
Mineral Bluff
Georgia 30559

Robin and Russ
Handweavers
533 North Adams Street
McMinnvills
Oregon 97128

Some Place
2990 Adline Street
Berkeley
California 94703

Osma G. Todd Studio
319 Mendoza Avenue
Coral Gables
Florida 33134

The Unique And Art Lace
Cleaners
5926 Delman Boulevard
St Louis
Missouri 63112

Van Scriver Bobbin Lace
130 Cascadilla Park
Ithaca
New York 14850

The World In Stitches
82 South Street
Milford
N.H. 033055

Australia

Dentelles Lace Supplies
3 Narrak Close
Jindalee
Queensland 4074

The Lacemaker
94 Fordham Avenue
Harrwell
Victoria 3124

Spindle and Loom
Arcade 83
Longueville Road
Lane Cove
NSW 2066

Tulis Crafts
201 Avoca Street
Randwick
NSW 2031

Belgium

't Handwerkhuisje
Katelijnestraat 23
8000 Bruges
Belgium

Kantcentrum
Balstraat 14
8000 Bruges

Manufacture Belge de
Dentelle
6 Galerie de la Reine
Galeries Royales St Hubert
1000 Bruxeiles

Orchidee
Mariastraat 18
8000 Bruges

Ann Thys
't Apostelientje
Balstraat 11
8000 Bruges

France

Centre d'Initiation à la
Dentelle du Puy
2 Rue Duguesclin
43000 Le Puy en Velay

A L'Econome
Anne-Marie Deydier
Ecole de Dentelle aux
Fuseaux
10 rue Paul Chenavard
69001 Lyon

Rougier and Ple
13–15 bd des Filles de
Calvaire
75003 Paris

West Germany

Der Fenster Laden
Berliner Str 8
D 6483 Bad Soden
Salmunster

P.P. Hempel
Ortolanweg 34
1000 Berlin 47

Heikona De Ruijter
Kloeppelgrosshandel
Langer Steinweg 38
D4933 Blomberg

Holland

Blokker's Boektiek
Bronsteeweg 4/4a
2101 AC Heemstede

Theo Brejaat
Postbus 5199
3008 AD Rotterdam

Magazijn *De Flijt*
Lijnmarkt 48
Utrecht

Switzerland

Fadehax
Inh. Irene Solca
4105 Biel-Benken
Basel

New Zealand

Peter McLeavey
P.O. Box 69.007
Auckland 8

Sources of Information

The Lace Guild
The Hollies
53 Audnam
Stourbridge
West Midlands
DY8 4AE

The Lace Society
Linwood
Stratford Road
Oversley
Alcester
Warwickshire
BY9 6PG

The British College of Lace
21 Hillmorton Road
Rugby
Warwickshire
CV22 5DF

The English Lace School
Oak House
Church Stile
Woodbury
Nr Exeter
Devon
EX5 1HP

International Old Lacers
President
Gunvor Jorgensen
366 Bradley Avenue
Northvale
NJ 076647
United States

United Kingdom Director
of International Old
Lacers
S. Hurst
4 Dollius Road
London
N31 RG

Ring of Tatters
Mrs C. Appleton
Nonesuch
5 Ryeland Road
Ellerby
Saltburn by Sea
Cleveland
TS13 5LP

Books

The following are stockists of the complete Batsford/Dryad Press range:

Alby lace Museum
Cromer Road
Alby
Nr Avisham
Norfolk NR11 7QE

Bridge Bookshop
7 Bridge St
Bath
Avon BA2 4AS

Creative Crafts
11 The Square
Winchester
Hants

Creative Crafts &
Needlework
18 High St
Totnes
Devon TQ9 5NP

Embroidery Shop
51 William St
Edinburgh
Lothian EH3 7LW

Foyles
119 Charing Cross Road
London
WC2H 0EB

Doreen Gill
14 Bamfield Road
Petersfield
Hants GU31 4DQ

The Handicraft Shop
47 Northgate
Canterbury
Kent

F. Herring & Sons
High West St
Dorchester
Dorset DT1 1UP

Dennis Hornsby
149 High St
Burton Latimer
Kettering
Northamptonshire
NN15 5RL

Honiton Lace Shop
44 High St
Honiton
Devon EX14 8PS

Loricraft
19 Peregrine Way
Grove
Wantage
Oxon

Tim Parker (Mail Order)
124 Corhampton Road
Boscombe East
Bournemouth
Dorset BH6 5NL

Ruskins
27 Bell St
Romsey
Hants

Sebalace
Waterloo Mill
Howden Rd
Silsden
West Yorks BD20 0HA

Arthur Sells
Lane Cove
49 Pedley Lane
Clifton
Sefford
Bedforshire SG17 5QT

Shireburn Lace
Finkel Court
Finkel Hill
Leeds
West Yorks
LS25 6EA

Waterstone & Co.
236 Union St
Aberdeen
AB1 1TN

Waterstone & Co.
4-5 Milsom St
Bath BA1 IDA

George White
40 Heath Drive
Boston Spa
LS23 6PB

Index